ENGLAND'S
FIRST CASTLE

The past which a historian studies is not a dead past, but a past which in some sense is still living in the present. But a past act is dead, i.e. meaningless to the historian, unless he can understand the thought that lay behind it.

E.H. Carr, *What is History?*

ENGLAND'S FIRST CASTLE

THE STORY OF A 1000-YEAR-OLD MYSTERY

TERRY WARDLE

Dedicated to my family

Cover illustrations: Front, the reconstructed early Norman castle at Saint Sylvain D'Anjou. Back, King Cnut and Queen Emma, see p.44.

First published 2009

The History Press
The Mill, Brimscombe Port
Stroud, Gloucestershire, GL5 2QG
www.thehistorypress.co.uk

British Library Cataloguing in Publication Data.
A catalogue record for this book is available from the British Library.

ISBN 978 0 7524 4797 1

Typesetting and origination by The History Press
Printed in Great Britain

Contents

List of Illustrations

Preface

This book is based on my search for the first castle in England, that is, the first castle built in England by a Norman, since professional historians, despite their usual squabbles and endless reservations, have generally agreed that castles as we know them were brought to this country by the Normans.

It was while researching a book on castles in my home county, Herefordshire, that I became aware of the total confusion over the dating and location of this first castle. Virtually nothing was known about it, despite a basis of evidence from the chroniclers, and its supposed location, which had been accepted for more than 100 years, seemed wrong, and was to prove so.

It seemed to me that this was an important subject and therefore one on which someone should carry out research. At that time I knew very little about Anglo-Saxon England and nothing about the sources for the history of the period, and I was therefore uniquely unqualified to carry out this task. Unfortunately it became clear that for more than a century no professional historian had shown any interest in the subject, preferring to regard the discovery of new castle sites as a task for the 'narrow specialization' of archaeology, as R. Allen Brown described it contemptuously in 1970, while they concentrated on the discussion of the castle and its relation to feudalism, and so on. Clearly it is important for historians to use archaeological evidence in the formulation of general theories, but it is important also for historians to look back at the evidence, if any, for past theories which they continue to repeat uncritically. In the end I took on the task because I felt certain that someone should, and there did not seem to be anyone else likely to.

I do not claim to have discovered England's first castle in the archaeological sense, since unfortunately archaeology cannot at present differentiate between the site of a castle built 15 years before the Norman Conquest and one built 15 years after it, or 50 years after it for that matter, but if there is evidence pointing to the existence of this castle, which there is, then it seems worthwhile to me to follow where that evidence leads, and that is what I have done.

Having carried out the initial research and formulated my ideas, I tried them out in a draft academic paper, and grateful thanks are due to all the scholars who kindly agreed to read it and offered valuable suggestions and criticisms, especially Dr Derek Renn, Mr Bruce Coplestone-Crow and Professor Frank Barlow. I have sometimes had the temerity to disagree with these distinguished scholars and historians, but aspects of my research have greatly benefitted from their generous advice and criticism, though any errors remaining are mine alone. Thanks are also due to the many historians identified in the Notes and Bibliography whose works I have consulted in preparing this book.

I have not attempted to establish any consistent rules for spelling of eleventh-century names used in the book, but have preferred to take a common-sense approach to obtain the simplest usage. So names which will already be familiar to readers in a modern form, such as Edward and Alfred, are used in that form; less familiar names are mainly given in the form used in Sir Frank Stenton's *Anglo-Saxon England*.

Terry Wardle
Worcester
August 2008

A Note on Sources

Eleventh-century specialists will already be familiar with many of the sources used in the preparation of this book. This note is intended to provide general information on some of the key sources for those who are not specialists on this period. Full publication details are given in the Bibliography. If a more detailed general bibliography of the period is required an excellent source is *Anglo-Saxon Studies: A Select Bibliography* (C.P. Biggam) at http://bubl. ac.uk/docs/bibliog/biggam.

Primary sources

Anyone working outside the major centres of learning is forced to rely on published sources, but fortunately many of the main primary sources for this period have been published in translation. All contemporary accounts of eleventh-century events were written by monks, who would have been the only ones with sufficient learning; usually they were working in the monasteries, though some monks were attached to courts or great households. With no printing, books had to be laboriously copied out by hand in the monastic scriptoria, but that did not prevent some titles being widely circulated and becoming, in effect, the bestsellers of their age. The output of monastic writers useful to historians included chronicles, histories, biographies and accounts of leading families, but the quality of this output varied widely. Some works of historians and annalists are still highly regarded for their objectivity, but in other cases writers were paid for their work and it undoubtedly sometimes reflected the prejudices and preconceptions of their patrons.

The key source for the period is a work which did not actually exist in its present form in the eleventh century and is known to us as the *Anglo-Saxon Chronicle* or *Chronicles*. The *Chronicle* as we have it is a compilation of a number of monastic chronicles deriving from various sources, nearly all written in Anglo-Saxon, or Old English as we know it. From about the late ninth century monks in various parts of the country, apparently inspired by Alfred the Great's encouragement of learning, began to record past and current events. Often these might be events relating to their monastery or to the church in their district, but some accounts of political and social events in the wider world were also included. It is by no means certain that all events were recorded as they occurred, but they were usually written down within a few years. These chroniclers did not share the historian's mission to explain; their task was only to record, which they often did with infuriating brevity and sometimes also lack of clarity, but their work is nevertheless the source from which our knowledge of the period primarily flows. The *Chronicle* material is drawn from a number of annals, written in the monasteries of Winchester, Abingdon, Canterbury, Peterborough, Worcester and elsewhere. These chronicles were circulated between monasteries so that any one monastery library had a wide range of chronicle material from which an annalist could work, to amend or add to his own chronicle.

Translations of individual chronicles were being printed at least as early as the seventeenth century, and there were several nineteenth-century editions featuring two or more chronicles paralleled, but nothing in the twentieth century until the 1950s brought a sudden flurry of activity. In 1952 a reprint was issued of an 1890s edition by Plummer of two of the chronicles parallel. In the following year G.N. Garmonsway produced a much-underrated edition of the main chronicles paralleled, the second edition of which, in 1954, took account of material from a number of chronicle scholars including Dorothy Whitelock, who published her chronicle material in the volumes of English Historical Documents in 1955. Whitelock's 1961 *Chronicle*, with D.C. Douglas and S.I. Tucker, seems to me to owe something in terms of layout to Garmonsway, but has often been preferred by scholars because it is slightly later. Both books use the title, *The Anglo-Saxon Chronicle*. The most recent translation, published as *The Anglo-Saxon Chronicles*, by Michael Swanton, was printed in a revised paperback edition in 2000. All the works mentioned have introductions giving further information on the complex history of the chronicle materials. Sadly no Anglo-Saxon–modern English version of all the chronicles paralleled is generally available at present.

We know that the range of chronicle material in existence was much wider than that which we now have because of a twelfth-century chronicle by a Worcester monk, originally identified as Florence, and published under his name up to the end of the nineteenth century, but more recently identified as John. This chronicle was written up to the death, at about 1118, of Florence, who is now regarded only as an assistant to the true writer, and was continued up to 1141 by John. The writer's intention was, in part, to make the chronicles more widely available by translating them from Anglo-Saxon into Latin, the most widely known language amongst the educated of that time, but this work is extremely valuable today because it preserves much chronicle material which is otherwise lost to us. The controversy about its authorship – one of those often barren 'either-or' arguments which professional historians nevertheless love to engage in – seems to have begun with a lengthy paper by chronicle scholar Sir Henry Howorth in *The Archaeological Journal* in 1916 (vol LXXIII no. 1-4), insisting that John was the real author. The evidence is inconclusive and hopefully historians may eventually come to the obvious common sense conclusion – supported by John himself – that both John and Florence were engaged in the preparation of most of the chronicle. In the meantime, the title of the chronicle will depend on the budget available. A major problem for anyone outside academia wishing to obtain this and other sources referred to below is that many of the latest editions are so expensive; this is certainly true of the three-volume edition of *The Chronicle of John of Worcester*, published by Oxford University Press in the 1990s. A much lower cost alternative is the series of editions of the Victorian translation by Joseph Stephenson, reprinted by various publishers over the years and in the 1990s by Llanerch Press of Lampeter – in this case under the title *The Chronicle of Florence of Worcester*.

Both the *Anglo-Saxon Chronicle* and the *Chronicle of John of Worcester* are valuable direct sources for the history of England's first castle. There are other contemporary or closely contemporary sources, including a number of histories, which contain little or no direct evidence but have been invaluable in piecing together information about the people and events of the period.

From an early stage historians were putting the *Chronicle* material to good use, but they also combined it with material from other sources, some of which may since have been lost, and from the strong oral tradition which existed amongst a largely illiterate population, which doubtless often included anecdotes that could not readily have been repeated publicly during a monarch's lifetime. We can never be certain that these oral traditions are entirely reliable, but they often provide information which can be found nowhere else, and they have largely been accepted by modern historians.

Among the first of these historians was William of Malmesbury, a monk who may have been born in Wiltshire and was of mixed Norman and Saxon parentage. His history of the kings of England was written in the first half of the twelfth century, possibly before he wrote a history of his own times which commenced in 1126. This means that he was possibly writing only about 70 years after some of the events described in this book, and was able to include information he had obtained from people who had first-hand knowledge of mid eleventh-century events. His *Gesta Regum Anglorum* ('The Deeds of the Kings of England') was reprinted by Oxford University Press in 1998. His many other books, mostly not yet generally available, include *Gesta Pontificum Anglorum* ('The Deeds of the Bishops of England') which can be a useful source; it was recently published under its Latin name in a typically expensive OUP two-volume edition, but the first translation, by David Preest, published in 2002 under the modern English title, is still available in an inexpensive paperback edition. At much the same time Henry, Archdeacon of Huntingdon, was also producing a valuable history, completed before 1135, and was the first writer to mention several anecdotes, including that of Cnut and the waves, which were no doubt collected from oral tradition and have gone on to become an established part of our historical record. His *History of the English People* was reprinted in the usual expensive edition by Oxford University Press in 1996, but a modern English translation covering only the period around the Conquest was published in a low-cost paperback (*Henry of Huntingdon: The History of the English People 1000-1154*) in 2002: now why can OUP not do that with all the other sources listed here?

The other great historian of that time was Orderic Vitalis, an English monk from Shrewsbury, who spent his life from the age of 10 at the Norman monastery of St Evroul, though he gives an account of visiting Worcester and meeting the chronicler John. Of Anglo-Norman parentage like William of Malmesbury, he wrote between 1114 and 1141, but from his European vantage point his interest in pre-Conquest England was inevitably less than that of William and Henry. His *Ecclesiastical History* was published by Oxford University Press in six volumes; vol II which relates to the period covered in this book was published in paperback with revisions in 1990. Because all these works are chronologically ordered it has not generally been thought necessary to include page references for them, or to indicate where information is based on the *Chronicle* or John of Worcester, since generally it is, unless otherwise indicated. At the same period Simeon, a monk of Durham, was also writing a history of the kings of England and slightly later historians included Roger de Hoveden and Roger of Wendover. There are also Scandinavian sources which are useful for their information on the Danes in England and Normandy, but none of these are widely available. There are also other medieval histories which may occasionally touch on a person or event relevant to the period dealt with here, but again sadly they are not widely available, though hopefully more such works will become readily available in the future.

Other contemporary sources have valuable material, though they may not always be entirely trustworthy. The *Encomium Emmae Reginae* was a work commissioned by Emma of Normandy in praise of herself and her late husband Cnut, possibly to try to influence political events after Cnut's death in 1035. It was apparently written by a monk at the Flanders monastery of St Bertin, probably about 1041-2, and in part provides a fairly objective account of the Anglo-Danish wars which led to the settlement with Edmund, probably based on *Chronicle* material. It also gives a very fanciful, and undoubtedly untrue, account of the events leading to Emma's marriage to Cnut, while her first husband, Aethelred, is pretty much written-out of history. The *Encomium* continues down to about 1041, where it ends with Edward's return to England, and was apparently written within a few years after that. The recent, comparatively inexpensive, reprint with the 1949 translation, published by Cambridge University Press in 1998, contains the original detailed introduction by Alistair Campbell and a modern introduction by Simon Keynes, which provide a detailed analysis of the *Encomium*'s historical strengths and weaknesses and much other valuable material. The *Vita Edwardi Regis* or 'Life of King Edward who rests at Westminster', written by a monk of St Bertin about 1066, is another commissioned work, written at the behest of Edith, widow of Edward the Confessor and sister to the ill-fated Harold Godwineson. In consequence it gives a perhaps unduly sympathetic account of Godwine's family and the events in which they were involved, but again the volume also contains a detailed introduction, by translator Frank Barlow, addressing these issues.

Also valuable is Kevin Crossley-Holland's *The Anglo-Saxon World*, an unrivalled source-book containing a wide range of Anglo-Saxon translations, recently published in an inexpensive Oxford World Classics edition.

The great eleventh-century land survey Domesday Book has appeared in various editions over the centuries and new translations were a particular feature of the Victoria County History volumes of the late nineteenth and early twentieth centuries. In the early 1990s a series of Alecto Editions volumes were published, featuring the original text and updated versions of the VCH translations. The translations only were subsequently published by Penguin as a single, relatively inexpensive, volume covering the whole country. Anyone wishing to study a particular county more closely will find the inexpensive Phillimore Latin–modern English volumes in their *History from the Sources* series indispensable. The volumes utilise the 1783 Latin text printed by Abraham Farley, with updated translations, detailed notes and supporting information. The volume on Herefordshire referred to in this book is No. 17 in the series.

Anglo-Saxon charters recording land transactions were invariably signed by a range of witnesses, and consequently are an invaluable source of information about titles, relationships, land ownership and much else which was often not otherwise recorded. There have been various standard collections of charters in the past but none are readily available and publication of previously unpublished charters, as well as continuing research on those already in publication, has led to a need for comprehensive renewal of the material available. The Joint Committee on Anglo-Saxon Charters was formed in 1966 by the British Academy and the Royal Historical Society, and is in the process of publishing a comprehensive 30-volume work, but probably more valuable to many researchers will be its searchable database at http://www.trin.cam.ac.uk/chartwww/charthome.html.

Secondary sources – Anglo-Saxons and Normans

The Norman Conquest and its aftermath has proved inordinately attractive to scholars and in recent years there has been greater interest in the Danish conquest, but Anglo-Saxon England has not proved as tempting and there is still no greater general survey than Sir Frank Stenton's *Anglo-Saxon England*, first published as long ago as 1943, though a third edition was produced in 1971, four years after the author's death. He is one of those rare historians able to demonstrate his exhaustive knowledge of the sources without detriment to the dramatic story he is telling. In some specialist areas, such as coinage, his work may now have been superseded, but as a general history of the period it is unequalled. Sadly, academics now seem to feel that the field is too broad to be encompassed by any one scholar, but, as his wife makes clear in the preface to the third edition, Sir Frank dedicated much of a 65-year career to this one volume. More recent is *The Anglo-Saxons*, containing articles by several distinguished scholars, which is a useful introduction to the period with the wealth of illustrations not to be found in Stenton's book, and *The Blackwell Encyclopaedia of Anglo-Saxon England*, edited by an impressive team of scholars, is a very useful though not exhaustive reference work.

There are many works on individual figures from pre-Conquest eleventh-century history. *Aethelred II: King of the English 978-1016* by Ryan Lavelle is an attempt to revise the fairly low opinion historians have traditionally held of this Anglo-Saxon monarch. Aethelred's young bride, Emma, has recently featured in several volumes; the pick of these is *Queen Emma and Queen Edith: Queenship and Power in Eleventh Century England* which also features Edward the Confessor's bride, Edith. Emma also features in *Queen Emma and the Vikings* by Harriet O'Brien. The career of Emma's second husband is dealt with in *Cnut: England's Viking King* by M.K. Lawson. There are two recent histories of Queen Edith's powerful family: *The Godwins* by the acknowledged authority on eleventh-century history, Frank Barlow, and *The House of Godwine: The History of a Dynasty* by academic Emma Mason. The most widely respected life of Queen Edith's husband is Frank Barlow's *Edward the Confessor*, but it is not easy to get hold of and it would be nice to see a reprint. The life of the most famous of the Godwins was most recently recorded in *Harold: The Last Anglo-Saxon King* by Ian W. Walker, which attempts to discount some of the Norman-inspired myths about Harold.

The modern history of Norman Conquest publishing has to begin with E.A. Freeman's massive *History of the Norman Conquest of England* in five volumes plus another for the index, which was published from the late 1860s. Freeman's work is not now highly regarded, nor readily available, but did have the merit of giving thorough consideration to Anglo-Saxon England prior to the Conquest. Two modern works which follow this example are *The Norman Conquest: Its Setting and Impact* by Dorothy Whitelock, David C. Douglas, Charles H. Lemmon and Frank Barlow, and *The Feudal Kingdom of England 1042-1216* by Frank Barlow, but neither will be easy to get hold of. *Feudal England* by Freeman's great rival J.H. Round was published in 1895 and continued to be reprinted up to 1964. A book which looks at the Normans in their European context is *The Normans and the Norman Conquest* by R. Allen Brown, while David Crouch focuses more sharply on Norman leadership in *The Normans: The History of a Dynasty*; Christopher Gravett and David Nicolle focus on military skills in *The Normans: Warrior Knights and Their Castles* and M.K. Lawson surveys the relative military strengths and weaknesses of the Anglo-Saxons and Normans in *The Battle of Hastings 1066*. Other works which may be cited by these authors are not always readily available; for example, Professor Crouch strongly recommends *Normandy before 1066* by David Bates, published in 1982, but it is now out of print and impossible to obtain.

A useful recent survey of the history and archaeology of Vikings in England is *Viking Age England* by Julian D. Richards. The volumes of the Victoria County History series, which began to appear in the late nineteenth and early twentieth century, should be a vital resource for any local historian, and often also provide valuable insights on national history. The older volumes may now have been superseded in some areas but their exhaustive surveys of historical evidence across the centuries are still invaluable. It is surprising how often even professional historians fall into errors which they could have avoided by consulting the relevant VCH.

Secondary sources – Norman castles

There is arguably no area of historical study which has led to greater controversy than that of Norman castles. Many of the controversies of the nineteenth century have since been resolved and a classification of ancient sites has been established but is by no means permanently fixed and this area of study is continually evolving.

The earliest twentieth-century work, which influenced generations of scholars, was *The Early Norman Castles of the British Isles* by Ella S.Armstrong, containing much material which was new at that time. Some of Mrs Armitage's work was reappraised in the light of subsequently discovered evidence in Derek Renn's *Norman Castles in Britain* in the late 1960s, though Dr Renn's work did not focus purely on early castles, so he did not follow up on Mrs Armitage's study of early earthworks. Dr Renn's book has to be regarded as the most up-to-date general survey of the field, though copies are not readily available and 40 years on a new general survey, taking account of the wealth of more recent evidence, is badly needed. *Timber Castles* by Robert Higham and Philip Barker has been the standard work on its subject since its first publication in 1992 and is likely to remain so for many years to come. Its study of earthworks makes it the true successor to Mrs Armitage, but the authors obviously did not intend to follow up her work on early castles, other than those of timber. Royal castles are dealt with in admirable detail in *The History of the King's Works*. Medievalist R. Allen Brown argued that a proper history of castles needed to take account of the social and economic significance of their construction and use, and in the early 1960s he produced a slim volume, *English Castles*, which he referred to as 'a tentative reconnaissance towards the ideal'. This is simply a brief summary of the publications which seem to me to be important in a field of history which has probably seen more written about it than any other.

Introduction

In early September 1051 the *Anglo-Saxon Chronicle*, that most eccentric but essential diary of our history before the deluge of 1066 overwhelmed English society and culture, recorded that the French had built 'aene castel' on the lands of the most powerful family in England. Did the monastic chronicler understand the full significance of what he had written? Surely not. For that he would have needed visionary powers. What he had briefly recorded was the building of the first Norman castle to be seen in England.

Within a few years the Norman conquerors of England would begin construction in earnest, throwing up, across several centuries, everything from modest knights' castles to giant fortresses, built to subdue the natives and protect the builders; alien constructions which dotted the captive landscape of England and Wales. Today the ruins of Norman castles provide a rich heritage which few of us will not have visited at some point, but the first castle referred to by the chronicler in 1051 was built 15 years *before* the Norman Conquest and a Norman castle had never previously been seen in the land. Almost 1000 years later we still know virtually nothing of that first castle and no-one has ever before attempted to unravel the mysteries surrounding it.

In common with many of the *Chronicle*'s enigmatic entries, the notation for 1051 posed more questions than it answered. For a start, what was the name of the castle builder? We had to wait for later *Chronicle* entries to discover that he was a Norman named Osbern, and even then we knew nothing about what he was doing invading England 15 years too early for the Conquest, building a castle on the lands of a powerful family who had no love for Normans. Osbern's reasons for being in England are not known beyond doubt, but he was probably one of those younger sons that Normandy sent out in some numbers in the eleventh century to seek their fortunes by the sword in foreign fields across Europe and beyond. What was this apparently unknown Norman doing in England at that time, and why did he build the castle which gave him a unique place in English history?

The *Chronicle* gave no indication of why he had built his castle just at that moment, but it was hardly an auspicious time for new building projects, with England on the brink of civil war. The king and perhaps the most powerful family ever known in Anglo-Saxon England had been locked for a decade in a bruising power struggle which had finally broken out into armed confrontation, and the nation was on the verge of self-destruction through massive civil slaughter. This dreadful confrontation may have been the inevitable consequence of long-standing, simmering resentments, but there is also evidence to suggest that it was the result of a regal plot which had gone disastrously wrong. What was the significance of the building of Osbern's castle just at this time? Was his castle building monumentally ill-timed, or did the fast-moving events of early September 1051 provide the motive behind it? These are questions which the *Chronicle* entry cannot answer, and only a detailed examination of the events of that autumn and their origins can begin to reveal Osbern's intentions.

Nor did the *Chronicle* entry tell us exactly where his castle was. The only exact locations we have ever previously been offered emerged from the works of two feuding Victorian academics, were not backed wth any evidence, and were undoubtedly wrong. Other than these somewhat eccentric contributions, the history of England's first Norman castle has remained a mystery for almost 1000 years.

So who was Osbern, why did he build the first castle in England in 1051, what was it like, and where exactly was it? To begin to answer these questions, and follow Osbern's footsteps as he strides boldly into the annals of English history, it is necessary to look back to the start of what would be a troubled century for England, at odds with itself and under siege from Scandinavian raiders, to try to understand the country in the eleventh century and to appreciate the widely varying origins and purposes of the many people – king, lords and commoners, Normans and Saxons – who would play their allotted parts in the dramatic events of 1051, that epoch-ending year after which, in certain important respects, England would never be the same again.

Chapter One

The Dawn of a
Troubled Century

Osbern undoubtedly never read the entries concerning him in the *Anglo-Saxon Chronicle*. It is improbable that he would have had any interest in them, even if he could read, and read Anglo-Saxon, which was very unlikely. As we will see later, he was likely to have been a warrior from a warrior culture and probably knew little of English history and cared even less, but he would surely have known the story, also retold in the *Chronicle*, of a remarkable woman who, like him, was a Norman. Her arrival in England in 1002 was to start a chain of events which ultimately led not only to the building of Osbern's castle but to the conquest of England by the Normans.

Ymma, or Emma as modern historians prefer to Anglicize her name, was the sister of Richard II, ruler of Normandy, and was probably born in the late 980s.[1] Their father, Richard I of Normandy, who died six years earlier, had enthusiastically fathered a whole dynasty of Norman nobles and consorts with two wives and various other ladies; in their case their mother was his second wife, Gunnor, a Danish woman, but Emma was apparently named after Richard's first wife, though what Gunnor had to say about that is not recorded. Richard's great-grandchildren included Henry I of England.[2]

The duchy Emma was leaving had grown from nothing in little more than three generations and it is ironic that modern translations of the *Chronicle* should refer to her countrymen as Frenchmen – the original mostly just referred to them as foreigners – since France as we know it did not exist. The Romans referred to what we call France as the kingdom of the Gauls, which tends to give us the impression that it was a nation state of long standing, but that was far from true. Gaul, long before the coming of the Romans, was inhabited by Celtic tribes linked by their common language rather than administrative structures, but as early as the third century the

area was being invaded by the Franks, Germanic tribes from the lower
Rhine region. With the end of Roman control in the fifth century the
Franks largely took power over the region and established a royal dynasty
of Merovingian kings of the Franks which survived until 751. In that year
the last of the Merovingian kings was deposed by the Carolingian dynasty,
the greatest of whose kings was Charlemagne. He conquered an empire
including modern France, Switzerland, Austria, Belgium, Holland, much
of Germany and parts of Italy and Spain. His influence extended across
Europe and east as far as the Elbe and beyond, though the empire did not
long survive his death in 814, threatened by power struggles from within
and attacks from without by Magyars and Saracens.

In 843 Charlemagne's grandson Charles the Bald became king, but the
empire of his grandfather had largely disintegrated into a series of regional
fiefdoms, leaving Charles ruling an area corresponding roughly with
modern France and almost constantly at war, mostly unsuccessfully, with
the Bretons and the people of Acquitane, as well as with his own brother,
Louis the German. After him the throne was lost to the dynasty for a while,
and when regained was held by a boy king, Charles the Simple, grandson
of Charles the Bald, and subsequently by a series of doubtful claimants.
The instability after Charlemagne inevitably created a political and military
vacuum which the seaborne opportunists of Scandinavia – at various times
Danes, Norwegians, Swedes and men from the outer islands, invariably
referred to collectively as Vikings, apparently from their word *vik*, a bay or
creek where they moored their boats – were only too ready to exploit to
their advantage. The history of Scandinavian expansion records attacks and
settlements across Europe from Dublin to Seville, as far north as Russia
and as far south as Morocco. The first recorded Viking attack on Frankish
territories may have taken place as early as 799, during Charlemagne's rule,
but he stiffened defences against the 'Northmen' and for almost 20 years
after his death there were no raids. After the fragmentation of his empire
the Vikings resumed and intensified their attacks, using the Seine, Loire
and Garonne to press home attacks on Rouen, Paris, Nantes and Toulouse.
Charles the Bald, characteristically incapable of defeating the raiders, bought
them off for a while with Danegeld, a form of tax payment.

It was about 911 when the founder of Normandy, leading a strong force
of young Danes, sailed up the Seine towards Rouen and into the French
history books. Traditionally these raids were for booty, including slaves,
that could be picked up and removed, but a new land hunger had become
evident; certainly other Vikings were seeking land in Frankish territories at
that time, though none were to do so as successfully as Hrolfr. His name was
probably pronounced Rolf, though it was Latinised by chroniclers to Rollo.
He was said to be the son of an earl of Orkney, and was known as the '*gongu*'

or 'walker' since it was said he was so tall that no horse was big enough for him, though historical writer Eric Linklater has pointed out that Norwegian horses were probably no bigger than Icelandic ponies of today,[3] rather than the somewhat larger animals found in the rest of Europe. Though it is likely he launched his attack on Rouen in 911, Scandinavian sources insisted Hrolfr had been fighting in Normandy since 898 and monastic historian Orderic Vitalis, a Shropshire-born monk at the later Norman abbey of St Evroul, writing in the early twelfth century, said he had defeated the duke of Orleans and the count of Bayeux, and besieged Paris for four years 'though by God's grace he never took it'.[4]

When Hrolfr and his men landed they found the countryside undefended and quickly pressed home their advantage by marching to Rouen and taking the town without too much difficulty. It was, said Orderic, 'dilapidated from generations of Viking attacks', and had actually been burnt down by Norse raiders in the time of Charles the Bald,[5] but it was an important and thus potentially wealthy trading centre, particularly for trade with the north. Rouen became the capital of Hrolfr's empire of Normandy. Soon afterwards, possibly in that same year, Hrolfr met Charles the Simple at St Clair on the River Epte, at the boundary between the Vexin and the district of Roumois, of which Rouen was the capital. There Hrolfr was ceded Rouen and the land to the west of it as far as Brittany, effectively Upper Normandy, which formed the nucleus of the future duchy. He was also given the king's daughter, Gisla, as his wife, even though he had apparently already married Poppa, daughter of the count of Bayeaux whom he had killed.

What was the reason for this sudden French generosity? From what little contemporary evidence exists, it seems likely that there were two reasons. Firstly the Franks wanted to mitigate the threat posed by Hrolfr. Orderic Vitalis wrote: '... in more conflicts than I can name he slowly crushed the Gauls and laid waste most of the country, burning and plundering as far as Burgundy.'[6] Perhaps just as important as buying off a Viking raider however, was encouraging one who showed promising signs of being a civilizing influence on his fellow raiders. Hrolfr had perhaps deliberately made himself 'the acceptable face' of Viking raiding. On taking Rouen the 'pagan' conqueror immediately established friendly relations with the archbishop there, thus winning a valuable ally and intercedent with the royal court. A leader of such good sense undoubtedly must have encouraged trade from Rouen, since it would be to his financial advantage. It is even said he embraced Christianity, at least in name.[7] A strong Danish Christian leader would be a valuable ally in 'civilizing' or combatting other Norse settlers.

Other grants of land followed in 924 and 933 to create Lower Normandy. Hrolfr's adaptation to Frankish ways was continued by his successors, adapting to local religion, laws and customs until, it has been said, they became more French than the French, though adaptation was something of a Scandinavian speciality; one nineteenth-century historian said: 'Danes who settled in England became Englishmen, Danes who settled in Gaul became Frenchmen'.[8] Despite this, it is likely that the Northmen – the name was gradually shortened to Normans – had to fight to consolidate and extend their territorial gains and were still doing so as late as the reign of William the Conqueror. During the reign of Duke Richard I, the third incumbent of Normandy, new Scandinavian settlers were invited into the duchy to help strengthen it, and Richard continued the policy of his predecessors, enhancing his power through the marital connections of his offspring.

It was this policy which brought Emma across the channel. Though probably barely in her teens, she was to marry the king of England. It was a diplomatic union and her husband-to-be was far from love's young dream. The Anglo-Saxon king, Aethelred II, youngest son of England's great law-giver, King Edgar, was already in his mid-thirties with a whole brood of children by his first wife, some of them as old as, or even older than, his new bride. She would hardly have been a welcome new arrival since her children would inevitably disinherit Aethelred's eldest sons, who would have grown up expecting to be in line to the throne. Emma however proved a redoubtable lady who married two kings of England and bred two others, including Edward the Confessor, who played a major role in the story of England's first castle.

Despite these achievements, Emma had long been a largely forgotten figure of English history, until the reappearance in the late 1990s of the *Encomium Emmae Reginae*, a contemporary tract in praise of her. Since then she has appeared in several books, including two published in 2005, in one of which – albeit a fictionalised version of events – Aethelred is accused of beginning their married life by effectively raping his teenage bride.

This is yet another example of the 'bad press' which Aethelred has unfailingly received down the centuries, perhaps largely because, like Macbeth, his reign began with a horrific murder which blighted it; though in Aethelred's case it was a murder of which he was almost certainly innocent. On the evening of 18 March 978 the young King Edward, Aethelred's half-brother, who may have been no more than 17 years old, arrived at Corfe Castle in Dorset for a friendly family visit with his step-mother Aelfthryth and his half-brother, then a boy aged about 10. Before he could dismount, said the *Chronicle*, the retainers welcoming him had surrounded Edward's horse and stabbed him to death. Even in an age when men 'were ready to tolerate any crime of frank violence',[9] this treacherous family murder was too much for people to stomach. The *Chronicle* abandoned its usual discursiveness over current affairs to record: 'No worse deed for the English was ever done than this was, since first they came to the land of Britain'.

The murder was undoubtedly committed to place Aethelred on the throne and it was inevitably conjectured that his mother, Aelfthryth, had planned it, but no-one was ever punished for the crime. Perhaps Edward had the last laugh. He came to be regarded as a saint and martyr, and his tomb at Shaftesbury became a place of pilgrimage for centuries after, while Aethelred became sovereign of a nation which had little respect for his legitimacy. 'Throughout his reign,' said eminent Anglo-Saxon historian Sir Frank Stenton 'he behaved like a man who was never sure of himself'.[10] This resulted in inept administration and ineffective military leadership, coupled with sporadic vicious acts of violence, one of which was to be Aethelred's undoing.

Later generations found fault with Aethelred even earlier in his life than the death of his half-brother. Influential twelfth-century historian William of Malmesbury recorded an anecdote he probably obtained from oral tradition, about Aethelred's baptism. During the event, which was well attended by senior churchmen, the infant was wholly immersed in the font, as was the practice at that time. To the horror of the watching bishops, the infant Aethelred 'defiled the sacraments by a natural evacuation'. Today the church has generally abandoned total immersion, and the reaction to any unfortunate incident during baptism would be largely down to the individual vicar's sense of humour, but such an incident in Aethelred's time was regarded as blasphemous. The presiding archbishop of Canterbury, the saintly Dunstan, is reported to have exclaimed: 'By God and his mother, this will be a sorry fellow!'

This story obviously only emerged some time after Aethelred's death and might be apocryphal, since he was hardly a popular figure, but clearly William believed it was true. Dunstan must have been less than delighted, 10 years after this unpleasant experience with one end of Aethelred's anatomy, to find himself placing the crown of England on the other end, and he is said to have warned the unfortunate new king during his coronation that the sin of Edward's murder: '... shall not be washed out but with much blood of the wretched inhabitants; such evils shall come upon the English nation as it hath never suffered'.

If by that Dunstan was referring to the depredations of the Vikings, there was not long to wait before his prophecy came true. The incursions began again in 991 with a raid on Kent by a marauder named Olaf Trygvason, a Christian convert who had spent his childhood and youth variously in exile in Sweden and as a slave in Russia, but who was to become king of Norway between 995 and 1000. By 997 the incursions had entered a new and more dangerous phase, with the arrival of a large fleet prepared to spend a number of years systematically plundering the wealthy coastal areas of southern England. Over the next two years they raided and ravaged in Cornwall, Devon,

Dorset, Somerset, South Wales, Hampshire, Sussex and Kent, before resting in Normandy for a year with their Scandinavian-turned-Norman cousins, which surely could only have taken place with the acquiescence of the duke.

In 1001 the Viking raiders were back and after another turbulent year for southern England Aethelred finally bought them off for £24,000 – raised by swingeing taxes – in the spring of 1002. In the dearly bought interim he desperately needed to find a way to deny Norman anchorages to future raiders. There had been a previous treaty of 991 with the duchy which had never proved effective and, though no accounts of the marriage negotiations exist, it seems certain that this time Aethelred wanted a much stronger tie to Normandy than a mere treaty, hence the royal wedding. There was also good reason for the Normans to seek a bond with England. Even when ravaged by the scourge of Viking raids, the land to which Emma had come was, by any test, a leading European nation, with a long if chequered history, which may be useful to relate here.

Anglo-Saxon England had its origins within a few decades of the departure of the last Roman legions, about the end of the fourth century. Britain had already been suffering raids since the 360s, by the Picts and Scots from the north, and in the south, by the Germanic Saxons from across the North Sea. What little evidence there is from this period suggests that the former Roman province had descended into a series of squabbling petty kingdoms, and war and famine were decimating the population, which at that time was probably only equivalent to the population of present-day Bristol.[11] The fifth-century resettlement, a conquest by any other name, is invariably ascribed to the Angles and Saxons, who are both regarded as Germanic peoples, but Angeln or Angulus, the land of the Angles, is in fact the neck of land between Germany and Denmark, and the Jutes came from Jutland, which is part of modern Denmark, home to later Viking raiders. The three peoples were clearly closely related, and the account of the great eighth-century English historian Bede[12] shows that ironically the invaders were originally invited here by the Britons.

In 443 a final desperate plea was made for help from the Roman legions in Gaul, but they were busy trying to fight off Attila the Hun, so around 449 a British chieftain named Vortigern appealed to the Angles who brought three ships' companies to defend Britain, landing at Ebbsfleet in east Kent. Their considerable success in beating back the Picts was rewarded with the grant of the Isle of Thanet, but according to Bede, who may have been using sources since lost, the conquest of England had always been their true goal, and they subsequently allied with the Picts against the Britons. The Angles were soon sending back word that the country was fertile and the Britons were cowardly, which brought much larger forces of Angles, Saxons and Jutes to these shores, under the leadership of brothers known to history as Hengist and Horsa, though these were apparently just nicknames, meaning 'stallion' and 'horse'. 'It was not long,' said Bede, 'before such hordes of these alien peoples vied together to crowd into the island that the natives who had invited them began to live in terror.' The invaders quickly began to take over but they did not have it all their own way. A Roman named Ambrosius Aurelianus, perhaps a survivor from the fighting in Gaul, galvanized the Britons into action and they beat the invaders and killed Horsa at Aylesford, Kent, in 493, winning a further victory at an otherwise unknown location named as Mount Badon about 500. It is to this period that the hard-won victories of the legendary British warrior King Arthur belong, though there is no record of him in Bede's account or any contemporary source; mysteriously he did not first appear in literature until the ninth century.

Initially the invaders' advance moved mainly up the eastern side of England but the Britons were steadily pushed back westward into Wales and the Cornish peninsula, and within a century of the British victory at Mount Badon the invaders were in control of England. The country was divided into seven kingdoms which formed the basis of administration of England throughout Anglo-Saxon rule, and echoes of them are still to be found today. The Jutes held just one of these kingdoms, while the Saxons and Angles each held three though the actual size of the territory they controlled was very different. The Juteish tribe of Cantware held the kingdom of Kent and gave their name to Canterbury. In addition, the Juteish tribe of Wihtware held the Isle of Wight and an area opposite on the mainland, in what would become Hampshire, though this was apparently never a separate kingdom. The Saxon tribes created three kingdoms; of the West Saxons (Wessex), stretching roughly from London to the edge of Cornwall, the South Saxons (now Sussex) and the East Saxons (now Essex). The bulk of the territory however was taken by the Angles, whose descendants were the East Angles of East Anglia, the Middle Angles of the kingdom which became known as Mercia and took in a large swathe of central England, and the people of Northumbria, which ultimately took in all of northern England. Bede said so many Angles emigrated to Britain that their original homeland was still unpopulated in his day. The line between invaders and defenders was not always clearly drawn. There is evidence that Britons persisted on the lighter soils of the uplands while Anglo-Saxons, preferring clay soils for their ploughs, populated the valleys. Intriguingly, Cerdic, the mythical founding king of the Saxon kingdom of Wessex, was apparently a Celt, and it has even been suggested that he was the leader of a joint Saxon/British group.[13]

Initially Kent was the most powerful of the seven kingdoms, under the rule of Aethelbert, who had married the daughter of a Christian Frankish ruler. He forced the other kingdoms to acknowledge his overlordship, at least in theory, and established a code of law based on Frankish models. He was also the first of the 'English' kings to convert to Christianity, and in

597 welcomed St Augustine's mission, establishing Canterbury as the seat of the supreme churchman in England. However the other kingdoms were still expanding to the west and Northumbria became arguably the largest, also ruling the lowlands of Scotland from the Humber to the Forth, and its kings made themselves supreme in the seventh century. By the eighth century however, Mercia became the most important kingdom under the great Offa, who ruled over all of England south of the Humber and marked the boundary with the descendants of former Britons in Wales with a dyke or ditch, 64 miles long. Offa was also the first king to mint the silver pennies which were a staple of English coinage for the next 400 years, but the supremacy of Mercia did not long survive his death in 796.

Early in the ninth century Wessex, roughly taking in the land between the Thames and the Channel, including modern Berkshire, Hampshire, Wiltshire, Somerset, Dorset and Devon, was to become the most important of the Anglo-Saxon kingdoms and its rulers were ultimately to achieve what no other kingdom had succeeded in accomplishing – the true unification of England. It was achieved despite the threat from Viking raids which almost overwhelmed the whole country. When Alfred, the only one of our rulers to be awarded the honorific 'the Great', became king of Wessex in 871 there wasn't much of his kingdom left for him to rule, and he had to take refuge from marauding Vikings in the fens around Athelney in Somerset. From that base he set out to rally his forces and take the war to the Danes. The secret of his success was the ingenuity with which he overcame the obstacles faced by a king relying on a part-time army of peasant farmers who would down arms from time to time and go home to see to their crops.

Alfred established a network of fortified settlements, built up a force of skilled cavalrymen to augment the militia, and overcame his manpower problem by splitting the militia in two, so that he could always have half the available men in arms at any one time while the other half of his army tended their fields. He built ships to give his forces a seaborne capability – though most historians seem to regard it as something of an exaggeration to call him 'the father of the British navy' – and he was also responsible for a resurgence in learning, personally translating a number of Latin works into English. In seven years Alfred succeeded in forcing the Danes out of Wessex and within 15 years of his accession he was able to persuade them to accept a treaty creating the Danelaw, where the customary laws of the Danes were in force rather than the laws of the Anglo-Saxons. The mutual respect for each other's territory embodied in the treaty halted Danish expansion until Alfred's successors could follow his example and drive the Scandinavians further north.

By the tenth century England was the unified nation that Alfred the Great had made possible, though it was hardly a peaceful land. At the time of Alfred's death the Danes controlled half of England in the Danelaw, comprising the lands to the north and east of Watling Street, now the A5, including Yorkshire, East Anglia and parts of the central and eastern Midlands in the old kingdom of Mercia, as far south as Northamptonshire – the Danish-controlled 'Five Boroughs' of Leicester, Nottingham, Derby, Stamford and Lincoln show the wide spread of Danish territory – and it took his eldest son, Edward the Elder, most of his 24-year reign to force them back into the north of England in a series of determined campaigns which, for the first time, brought all of England under the direct control or influence of one man in the reign of Aethelstan, Alfred's grandson. The old seven kingdoms had now shrunk to four, East Anglia, Northumbria, Mercia and Wessex and although it was hardly the united realm that it later became, a good start had been made on the creation of England. In their realm, the rulers of England established efficient national and local government, which would be utilised by both Danish and Norman rulers during the course of the eleventh century.

The land of Bede of Northumbria and the West Saxon Aldhelm had long been famed for its learning: their works were used for centuries afterwards and Bede's history formed the basis of the earliest entries of the *Anglo-Saxon Chronicle* and many later histories. 'There were periods when the Anglo-Saxon contribution to learning, literature and art had been spectacular,' wrote eminent Anglo-Saxon scholar Dorothy Whitelock in a collection of essays commemorating the ninth centenary of the Battle of Hastings.[14] Another Anglo-Saxon scholar, Kevin Crossley-Holland, said they were: 'the most sophisticated pre-Conquest people in Europe and produced poems, illuminated manuscripts, jewellery and other artefacts of the very highest order'.[15] Eighth-century British missionaries to the Germanic tribes spread this high English culture and influence across Europe.

England was accounted a rich and fertile land by a Dane in Aethelred's service, and there was an agricultural surplus, especially of wool and cheese, to trade abroad. Fine embroidery and English metalwork were also in demand overseas, and England had traders in Rome while London hosted merchants from across Europe. York had a considerable trade with Scandinavia, Chester was the main trade route to Ireland and, then as later, Bristol traded slaves, even though the church frowned upon it.

Emma may have found the Anglo-Saxon world a little less strange than she might have expected, not least because of the long tradition of Scandinavian influence in Wessex. This influence extended to English culture: M.K. Lawson pointed out that Beowulf 'the most celebrated of all surviving Anglo-Saxon poems' is actually set in Denmark and southern Scandinavia and doesn't mention Britain at all.[16] One of Emma's biographers suggests that even the language may have been somewhat familiar to her, since in addition to Old French, Emma would have spoken Old Scandinavian, which 'was not entirely dissimilar to the Old English spoken by the Anglo-Saxons'.[17]

Emma arrived in the spring of 1002, so the marriage must have taken place no later than early summer; it was in no-one's interest to delay. Whether she made a beautiful bride is not known since there is no description of her wedding, and indeed no reliable description of her appearance. Given her Danish ancestry she might be expected to be tall and blonde, but the two known portraits of her are stylised affairs which show her muffled in voluminous gowns, with a head-dress covering her hair and part of her face, so there is little or nothing to be learnt from them. Her first child was born at Islip, near Oxford, and named Edward, probably after his father's saintly, murdered half-brother; perhaps showing Aethelred still trying to expiate the crime. The year is uncertain but was probably 1005, some three years after the marriage, suggesting that accusations of Aethelred's urgent conquest of his bride, while colourful and dramatic, are unlikely to be true. A daughter, Godgifu, and a second son, Alfred, were born between 1005 and 1013.

What Emma thought of Aethelred we don't know, but she refused to use the Saxon name he gave her, Aelfgifu; a perhaps less than diplomatic suggestion since it was the name of his first wife, although in fairness to Aethelred it should be mentioned that this was a 'royal' name, often given to brides marrying into the Wessex royal family. The chroniclers frequently referred to her by her 'official' name but in a contemporary source in her honour she is referred to only as Emma. Whether Aethelred was also unhappy with the match is unknown, but certainly gossip repeated by William of Malmesbury suggested that he often rejected his bride's bed and spent his time with 'harlots'. A Dane who spent some time in his service described him as 'a driveller … wholly given up to wine and women'. It's hard to imagine this determined woman had any great love for the man who was doomed to be known to history as Aethelred 'The Unready'. Even his nickname is a mistake; it's a mistranslation of the Anglo-Saxon 'unraed', which didn't mean unready but 'ill-advised'; a euphemism in past ages for incompetence in a monarch, implying that it was really his advisers who were being attacked. It was also a sarcastic Anglo-Saxon joke – Aethelred meant 'good counsel.' Nevertheless the marriage marked the first formal alliance between England and Normandy, and was the first of the links which would lead to William's invasion 64 years later.

The link to Normandy proved to have unexpected advantages for Aethelred and it might have served to help protect England from further Viking incursions, had it not been for the king's stupidity and viciousness. In November of that year Aethelred ordered the killing of all the Danes in England, men, women and children. The pretext for this act of savagery was a supposed plot by the Danes to kill the king and take power, but the motive was most likely revenge for the humiliation heaped on Aethelred by Viking raids. The massacre was to take place on 13 November, the feast day of St Brice, a fifth-century bishop of Tours whose name appeared in many early English church calendars and was still in the Book of Common Prayer in the Latinized form of Britius in the 1960s. Henry of Huntingdon, writing in the early twelfth century, said he had spoken in his youth to 'very old persons' – they must have been at least in their 80s – who gave him a detailed account of this 'flagrant outrage', as he called it:

> ... the king sent with secrecy into every town letters, according to which the English suddenly rose on the Danes, everywhere on the same day and at the same hour, and either put them to the sword, or, seizing them unawares, burnt them on the spot.

Sir Frank Stenton[18] pointed out that this order could not have been executed in one third of the country – York and Lincoln for example, were almost wholly Danish towns – but Danes were certainly slaughtered in Oxford and probably elsewhere, including Gunnhild, sister of King Swein Forkbeard of Denmark, with her husband Pallig and her son, who had been captured the previous year while raiding England. William of Malmesbury said Gunnhild, who 'possessed considerable beauty', saw 'her husband ... murdered before her face and her son, a youth of amiable disposition, was transfixed with four spears', before she was beheaded. Perhaps Aethelred believed that his new-found friendship with the Vikings-turned-Franks of Normandy would protect him from any consequences. If so, he was in for a very unpleasant surprise. Gunnhild's brother was a major force in Scandinavia; he not only ruled Denmark but also most of Norway, and he was a close ally of the king of Sweden. In the following year he raised a large force and sailed for England, undoubtedly intent on avenging his sister's killing. 'The fury of the Danes', said later historian Henry of Huntingdon, 'was inflamed like fire when any one should attempt to extinguish it with blood.'

The disembarked Danes were soon 'overspreading the country like a swarm of locusts', oppressing England 'with rapine and slaughter'. In that first year Swein's army sacked and burnt Exeter, Aethelred's ill-fated wedding present to Emma, and Wilton, and went as far as Salisbury – further inland than any raiding force had ever previously penetrated – before returning to their ships. It was the start of 13 years of almost continuous brutal warfare which would eventually see Emma and Aethelred driven out of England.

It is probably difficult for us to imagine, across the centuries, what these Viking raids must have been like for the people of villages and towns which fell victim to them, though we can gain some insight from the fervent Anglo-Saxon prayer: 'From the fury of the Norsemen, good lord deliver us'. There were earthworks and walled defences around many settlements, so many in fact that by the tenth century in some parts of the country, certainly in Wessex, no village was more than 20 miles from a defensive *burh*.[19] The quality of these defences could vary widely; some were based on Roman fortifications or Celtic earthworks, while others were fortified new towns such as Wareham, Cricklade and Wallingford, but the ferocity of Viking attacks often quickly surmounted these defences.

The ruthlessness of the raiders, sailing south for profit and barbaric pleasure, would have been exacerbated by the inherent warrior brutality of the age, and by a racial element somewhat akin to ethnic cleansing. Any finer feelings raiders may have felt would have been reserved for their own kind and, exceptionally, for those who showed extreme courage. Thus sympathy for ordinary people getting on with their everyday lives would have been incomprehensible to Viking raiders, who would have seen no moral objection to slaughtering foreign races down to the last man, woman, and child, and taking pleasure in doing so. That pleasure would certainly have included raping women 'sometimes by a dozen soldiers one after the other',[20] and inflicting painful mutilation and death on all who were not being taken away for sale as slaves. For the English of that time there was also the added horror that these attacks were being inflicted on Christians by heathens. Historian Orderic Vitalis emphasised this religious element: 'The Christian flock everywhere suffered in the storms, and falling a helpless prey to heathen wolves was cruelly torn to pieces by them'.[21] It probably seemed to the English though that these were simply the standards of an age in which blinding and mutilation were accepted punishments for English wrongdoers, and captured raiders could expect nothing better, and probably worse, than they might have meted out.

In 1004 East Anglia was battered by the raiders and in 1005 England was ravaged by a terrible famine. Whether this was, at least in part, caused by the depredations of the raiders or by natural factors is not clear, but it was, said the *Chronicle*, 'the most severe in living memory'. The deaths of people and of the livestock on which people relied for an important part of their sustenance, which resulted are nowhere recorded in the *Chronicle*, though realistically it is unlikely that there was any central collection of such information.

In the following year the raiders returned at midsummer and though a large force was assembled from southern and central England to oppose them, the Vikings evaded them and raided at will until the autumn, by which time the depredations of the Anglo-Saxon levies seeking supplies made the people wonder whether they weren't almost as bad as the raiders. In November the raiders retired to winter at their base on the Isle of Wight, but while the Anglo-Saxons celebrated Christmas the Vikings launched surprise attacks in the Home Counties, including the burning of the fortified town of Wallingford. In the new year Aethelred fell back on his usual solution and paid the raiders £30,000 or more to go away.

While Aethelred is hardly a sympathetic figure, in fairness he did make efforts to find a means of combating these raids, but his endeavours seemed always to be doomed to failure, as was amply demonstrated in the next two years. In 1008 Aethelred ordered that every part of England must urgently contribute to the building and equipping of a massive fleet, probably of about 300 ships. The strategy was clear: if the raiders couldn't be stopped once they were on shore, then they must be stopped before they landed. There were, said the *Chronicle*, more ships 'than there had ever been before in England in the days of any king.' By the following year the ships were built and the fleet was stationed off Sandwich, positioned to repel any force of raiders. For once Aethelred was truly ready. 'But,' said the *Chronicle*, 'no more than on previous occasions were we to enjoy the good fortune or the honour of naval operations which would be advantageous to this land.'

What went wrong, as on other occasions, was Aethelred's judgement. In 1007 he had decided to strengthen control of central England by reviving the title of earldorman or earl of Mercia. It was a sensible idea, but the man he chose for the role was a thegn named Eadric, who was to acquire an evil reputation for disloyal double-dealing in negotiations with the

1 Aethelred II and his son by his first marriage, Edmund Ironside. An engraving from *c.* 1850, based on coins from their reigns.

raiders, and the nickname '*Streona*' or 'acquisitor' for his purloining of church lands – and his brother was apparently little better. Before the raiders arrived, Beorhtric, Eadric's brother, went to the king and accused another commander, a Sussex thegn named Wulfnoth, of treason. There is no record of the charge and no knowing whether it was trumped up, but it was to sink Aethelred's fleet – literally. Wulfnoth – the father of Godwine, who probably did more than any other, albeit unintentionally, to bring about the building of England's first castle – was not waiting around to find out whether he would be found guilty of the charge. Showing the ruthless opportunism and charismatic leadership for which his son would later become justly famous, Wulfnoth persuaded the men of 20 ships to follow him and he deserted the king's fleet and set off on a series of piratical raids along the south coast. The ambitious Beorhtric, perhaps believing that Wulfnoth's capture could lead to a title comparable to his brother's, set off in pursuit with 80 ships, but before long, said the *Chronicle*: '... he was met by a storm worse than anyone could remember: the ships were all battered and knocked to pieces and cast ashore'. When the storm abated Wulfnoth's men turned up and burned the wreckage. One hundred ships short, and fearing the result if the raiders were now encountered, Aethelred and his senior commanders simply abandoned the fleet and went home. The crews then moved the remaining ships to the safety of London and – to complete the tragicomedy of that summer – shortly afterwards the Viking raiders arrived and took over the now-deserted anchorage off Sandwich.

A chronicler writing 16 months later said that since their return in 1009, when they had been joined by two new fleets commanded by Danish earl Thorkell the Tall and by Hemming, possibly his younger brother, the Vikings had ravaged all or part of 15 counties in southern and eastern England, not counting East Anglia which had been badly hit again, and there seemed no end to the agony. In 1011 they took Canterbury and captured the archbishop, Aelfheah, who was held for seven months. The *Chronicle* bewailed the failure to offer the raiders tribute in time, but southern England had been ravaged and despoiled of much of its wealth and it was 1012 before £48,000 was raised to persuade them to desist. A separate ransom was demanded for Aelfheah, but he refused to allow anything to be paid for him, and he was brutally murdered by Vikings during a drunken feast at Greenwich, apparently against the orders of their commander, Thorkell the Tall, who was said by a German chronicler to have offered everything he had except his ship to ransom the archbishop.[22] Whether because of his disgust at the murder or his distrust of the men who had committed it against his orders is not clear, but when the fleet returned to Scandinavia, Thorkell, with 45 ships, deserted and entered Aethelred's service. He was not the only Scandinavian fighting for England. Norwegian Olaf Haroldson, who took control of his native land during the later Danish campaign in England, had entered Aethelred's service at the time of Swein's invasion, and after a period fighting for Normandy, he joined the king on his return from exile in 1014.

England was now thoroughly demoralised. 'There was sufficient resilience in Old English society to repair even the heavy material damage suffered in these years,' said Sir Frank Stenton. 'But the ignominious collapse of the English defence caused a loss of morale which was irreparable.' Defeat now seemed inevitable and in the following year, '... on a people predisposed to accept humiliation the whole strength of the Danish kingdom fell.'[23]

This time the expedition was something more than a raid, even one designed to punish England for accepting the service of the traitor Thorkell. England's will to resist had been broken and there seemed no bar to Swein making himself king of England. By August 1013 Swein had arrived with his fleet off Sandwich, but instead of harrying the south as he had formerly done, he headed north to where there had been a large Danish population since the days of Alfred. He was not mistaken in his expectation of their loyalty to a Danish leader: the whole of the north quickly submitted to him, and he cautiously secured their loyalty by taking hostages from every area, before demanding horses and provisions for his men and heading south. The people of Oxford, which had been burnt down in 1009, submitted as soon as they saw Swein's force approaching and Winchester did likewise. After a disastrously unsuccessful attempt to take London, Swein turned west again and received the submission of the western nobility at Bath, after which London, standing out alone, submitted without a fight. Said the *Chronicle*: '... the whole nation accepted him as their undisputed king', and Emma was forced to flee to Normandy with her daughter and sons, Edward, now perhaps eight years old, and Alfred, followed soon afterwards by Aethelred, finding a refuge which would not have been available to him but for his marriage to Emma.

England was now firmly in Danish hands, and short of Swein dying, the luckless Aethelred had no hope of ever returning to his kingdom. Fortunately for him, that was exactly what happened in early February 1014. Swein had been laying siege to Bury St Edmunds, the site of the church containing the relics of Edmund, king of the East Angles, who was savagely executed about 869 by the sons of Ragnar Lothbrok, the legendary Viking leader said to have been thrown into a snake pit by the Anglo-Saxons. Swein disparaged Edmund's sanctity and demanded an 'enormous' tribute from the town, failing which he would destroy the martyr's church and torture the clergy. But, said John of Worcester, as he addressed his troops he saw St Edmund, fully armed, coming towards him. He called out for help but like Macbeth and Banquo's ghost at the feast, no-one else saw the apparition, which fiercely ran him through with a spear. He was taken to Gainsborough where, '... tormented with great pain until twilight, he ended his life with a wretched death on 3 February'.

The fleet chose as their new commander Swein's younger son Cnut, but he was then an inexperienced youth, unequal to the challenge. The way was now open for those English noblemen who had submitted to Swein through fear to restore Aethelred. We have no means of knowing what the former king felt about their pleas for him to return. Within 18 months he would be seriously ill and he may already have been suffering symptoms of that illness. He was secure in Normandy and had no need to subject himself once more to the tempestuous turmoil of early eleventh-century English politics. But he did. Whatever his motives – whether continued lust for power or dedication to his regal duty – Aethelred soon returned, and by April 1014 was leading an expedition to Lindsey, near Gainsborough, where the Danish fleet still rested. Hearing of the English approach, Cnut put to sea and returned to Scandinavia, leaving Aethelred to slaughter the local Danes who had harboured the fleet. Cnut's parting gesture was to put ashore at Sandwich the hostages his father had taken, after cutting off their hands, ears and noses. Some of these 'young men of great nobility and elegance' were also castrated, according to William of Malmesbury.

Cnut was not to be away long. Though his brother Harald had become king of Norway in his father's place, Cnut was allowed to recruit there, and with his powerful brother-in-law, Eric of Hlathir, the greatest nobleman in Norway, and Thorkell the Tall, once more changing sides, perhaps because of English treachery to his brother, he gathered a fleet and returned in September 1015. He was soon joined by the treacherous Eadric, who, for his personal profit, had probably covertly aided the Vikings virtually since being made earl, and largely helped frustrate attempts to defeat them on land. He brought with him 40 ships – those that Thorkell had taken over to the English – and boosted the Danish force by 1016 to a considerable 160 ships. Since each of these ships would probably have carried about 80 men,[24] the total force must have numbered about 13,000. Some men must have remained with the ships but this still provided a raiding party of more than 10,000 fighting men, and southern England was once more suffering the full force of their savagery.

By now Aethelred was terminally ill and responsibility for the fightback against the Danes rested on his second son by his first marriage, Edmund, nicknamed Ironside for his admired fighting qualities. Nevertheless, when the militia Edmund had raised refused to take the field unless the king was present, the ailing Aethelred valiantly turned out. By St George's day, 23 April, he was dead, after a 38-year reign marked by incompetency and disaster for England. 'The historians who regard Aethelred's reign as a time of national degeneracy have good contemporary opinion behind them,' wrote Sir Frank Stenton.[25] 'In a series of crises, each of which demanded a concentration of the national energy, the king could neither give direction to his people nor hold his greater subjects firmly to their allegiance.' A revisionist tendency has more recently emerged, represented by Aethelred's biographer, Ryan Lavelle, whose book on Aethelred praised the king's 'effective' use of Danegeld and his administration of the realm prior to 1013, but an objective reader might well find it hard to see Aethelred's reign as a success or view most of his judgements as anything other than disastrous for England.

The nation was now totally divided and at odds with itself. The men of London, and the noblemen who had taken refuge in the city from surrounding counties, chose Edmund as their new king, but within a few days a perhaps more representative assembly met at Southampton and chose Cnut. The stage was set for a dramatic showdown between these two combative, ambitious young men. During a summer of move and counter-move Edmund defeated the Danes several times, causing the treacherous Eadric to change sides once more back to the English, but during a potentially decisive battle at Ashingdon in south-east Essex, between the Thames and the Crouch estuary, Eadric fled with his forces, starting a general rout which left the field to Cnut. John of Worcester claimed Eadric had made a secret deal with Cnut.

Despite this victory, Cnut's advisors had no doubt that Edmund could raise further forces and continue the war, and Cnut's forces must have been badly depleted after a summer of warfare, so they sought a settlement with Edmund. The two men met on an island in the River Severn at Naight Brook, near Deerhurst in Gloucestershire, and agreed a deal in which Cnut would rule central and eastern England and London, and Edmund south-western England. With some noblemen controlling land in both areas this could have been a difficult compromise to enforce, but on 30 November 1016 Edmund suddenly died, or more likely, was murdered. There is no contemporary account of the cause of his death, and it was not until later that the accusation of murder emerged, but it must surely have been rumoured at the time; his death was just too convenient.

Henry of Huntingdon had a colourful story that when the king went 'to the house for relieving calls of nature', he was stabbed twice by an assassin secreted underneath in the pit, and the weapon was left 'fixed in his bowels'. The killer was said to be the son of the treacherous Eadric Streona, but when Eadric proudly announced the assassination to Cnut, so Henry's story goes, he was quickly decapitated and his head stuck on a pole on the highest battlement of the Tower of London. The latter part at least is untrue, since the *Chronicle* recorded him being given control of Mercia in 1017, though he was killed in London later that year; 'very justly' added one chronicler. Whoever committed the murder, it must surely have been on Cnut's order.

There were a number of valid claimants to Edmund's throne, including his own children and the other sons of Aethelred, but there was only one claimant with the power to enforce his claim. Cnut, the youth who, two years earlier, had clearly felt himself unequal to the task of commanding his father's forces in battle, now found himself undisputed king of England; the nation's first Viking king.

To Emma, probably taking refuge with her brother in Normandy, this year must have seemed the ultimate disaster. She began it as the Queen of England, with every hope that her sons might succeed to the throne. At its end however, she had no husband, no throne, no country and no hope of succession for her children. Yet the 'whirligig of time' still had undreamt fates to bring in for Emma and, more importantly, for her son in whose reign, and possibly at whose order, England's first castle was to be built.

Chapter Two

England Conquered

On 1 December 1016, the young Dane, Cnut, who had only joined his father's raiding forces for the first time three or four years earlier, was undisputed ruler of England. This was something more than a matter of mere territoriality. Cnut, whose name was formerly often Anglicized as it is pronounced, Canute, was the first Viking leader to be admitted into the 'civilized' fraternity of Christian European kings. A century earlier Cnut's countryman, Hrolfr, had begun his conquest of the Christian lands which would constitute the duchy of Normandy, but no 'heathen' Viking had ever become ruler of a major western European Christian nation. It should have been a daunting prospect for a young man who must have known little of England and its people, let alone of the governance of either, but if Cnut was overawed by the prospect there is little sign of it in contemporary sources.

He quickly, and ruthlessly, set about eliminating potential rival claimants and opponents with a mixture of political cunning and utter brutality. One of his first acts was to summon to London all the bishops, earls and other dignitaries who had witnessed the settlement with Edmund to divide the kingdom. When they were assembled, John of Worcester recorded that he cunningly asked them, 'as though in ignorance', whether the settlement had included any provision for Edmund's brothers or children to inherit his dominion. All assembled immediately answered that the settlement contained no such provisions, thus disinheriting at a stroke all of Edmund's kin of the Anglo-Saxon royal house. 'God knows,' said John, 'they bore false witness and lied deceitfully, thinking that he would show them favour and give them large presents in consideration of their lies.' No doubt there was a self-serving element to this 'political compromise', but the chronicler, writing from the safety of a century later, is perhaps being somewhat harsh. London would then have been under military occupation by the ruthless Danish army and any man returning an answer other than that which Cnut sought could expect little mercy. Even so, as the chronicler noted, 'some of these false witnesses were shortly afterwards slain'. But not before Cnut had required them to swear an oath of fealty to him, agree to raise taxes to meet the cost of maintaining his army and exile Edmund's highly-regarded brother Eadwig, a son of Aethelred's first marriage and the man around whom Anglo-Saxons were most likely to rally if they had any appetite for further bloodshed, which seemed doubtful.

Eadwig was the first of many to suffer at Cnut's hands, and exile was only the beginning; as a solution to the Eadwig problem the new king had in mind something altogether more permanent. Immediately after the assembly, Cnut reportedly summoned the duplicitous Eadric Streona and broached the subject of Eadwig's murder, once he was out of England. Eadric suggested that the man for the job was Aethelward, but though he subsequently agreed to carry out the crime, John of Worcester said he had no intention of doing so. Someone else did – probably Thorkell the Tall or one of his agents – and Eadwig was murdered a few months later, as was Aethelward; failing to carry out Cnut's wishes was a dangerous business. Cnut's biographer, M.K. Lawson, said Eadwig had returned from exile and may have been planning revolt when he was killed,[1] though he quotes no source; if the source was Scandinavian, which seems likely, this was probably nothing more than a later writer's attempt to mitigate or excuse Cnut's crime. Cnut even exiled another Eadwig, styled 'king of the peasants'; this appellation has never been explained but his obvious popularity was presumably sufficient to seal the fate of this individual, though John of Worcester said he was later reconciled to the king.

Edmund's two young sons, Edmund and Edward, who as grandsons of Aethelred and great-grandsons of Edgar should undoubtedly have succeeded to the throne, managed to survive, but not thanks to Cnut's mercy. Edmund married only in 1015 so his sons cannot have been more than babies and, unable to risk their murder in England, Cnut sent them to Sweden, requesting that they be put to death there, but the king instead sent them to the royal court of Hungary, where they were brought up beyond Cnut's reach. Edward subsequently married Agatha, a daughter of the brother of the emperor, Henry II, and was the father of Margaret, queen of Malcolm of Scotland, and grandfather to Edgar who, for a short time, was the rallying point for Anglo-Saxon opposition after the Conquest, though he was subsequently reconciled to the Conqueror and served him in several foreign adventures. Margaret's daughter, Edith-Matilda, married Henry I of England in 1100 and was grandmother of Henry II and a direct ancestor of all the Plantaganet kings of England. Thus Edmund Ironside's destiny, paralleling that of Banquo, was to become ancestor to a line of kings of England, though he never truly held the title himself.

John of Worcester recounted the violent events of Cnut's early reign but put much of the blame for them on the ill influence of Eadric Streona.

Even the *Encomium* which Emma later commissioned, which was also fulsome in its praise of Cnut, could not help but note: '... he ordered the execution of many chiefs,' though predictably it suggested that this was to punish their faithlessness to Edmund.[2] This is hard to accept however, since Cnut was about to confer new honours on the most faithless of them all, the duplicitous Eadric. Cnut's ruthlessness emphatically confirmed to the Anglo-Saxons that theirs was a conquered nation, and the message clearly struck home. When William of Normandy conquered England half a century later the Battle of Hastings was only the prelude to a series of campaigns to put down insurrections by the supposedly defeated Anglo-Saxons. There was no such aftermath to Cnut's defeat of Edmund at Ashingdon; in fact he was able to spend a good deal of his reign out of England without fear for the security of his rule. This might seem strange, since England had good reason to detest the Danes. Many a town and village had reason to recall with a shudder the depredations of the raiders, and leading families had brutally mutilated sons which served as a daily reminder of Cnut's ruthless barbarity, yet despite some rumblings of discontent, there was no major move to mount opposition to him. Perhaps in part this was because the nation's leaders had accepted Cnut as their ruler, with whatever degree of willingness; but probably more important to English acquiescence were the years of brutal raiding which had preceded his father's quest for power. It is hardly surprising that there seemed to be no appetite for renewed bloodshed, and if Danish rule of England was the price of peace then men were ready to pay it. Cnut gave an object lesson in how that peace would be defended, when a force of 30 imprudent Viking raiders sailed into English waters in spring 1018. He immediately set out with his fleet and destroyed them, both ships and ships' companies.[3]

Danish rule was not the 'culture shock' to the Anglo-Saxons that we might have expected. They had, as Cnut's modern biographer pointed out, 'always lived to a greater or lesser extent within a Scandinavian world'.[4] The language and culture of the Danes were familiar enough to the Anglo-Saxons; however that of the later Norman invaders – once Danes but then inveterate Francophiles – was to prove quite alien to England. There also seems to have been a quite different character to the two conquests. In the 1060s Norman knights largely supplanted Anglo-Saxon landholders, combining new civil rule with military occupation across the country. In contrast, though there does seem to have been some ceding of lands to major followers in Cnut's reign, it was nothing like the wholesale land grab after the Conquest. Military occupation, given the likely size of Cnut's army after Ashingdon, was probably confined mainly to London and perhaps some ports, and was not to last for long.

However conquest was not the only price the nation had to pay for peace: all England was subsequently required to assist in raising more than

£80,000 in tribute to support the Danish army that had conquered them.
Religious writers saw the Viking raids and the eventual Danish conquest
of England as God's punishment on the Anglo-Saxons, for sins which were
rarely specified, but probably chiefly comprised cowardice. Anglo-Norman
Henry of Huntingdon, shocked by Edmund's death, certainly saw the
raising of this massive tribute, which must have been a major blow to a
ravaged England, as God's judgement on the cowardly Anglo-Saxons: 'In
this way,' he wrote, 'the just Lord imposed on the English the tax-gatherer
they deserved'.

The lack of opposition to Cnut did not necessarily mean he had no
problems. Having seized power by the sword, his was the customary fate
of any usurper – only the faithless would hasten to serve him, and he was
therefore forced to place his trust in the inherently untrustworthy. His first
administrative act as king was to divide his new kingdom into four parts,
based on the ancient Anglo-Saxon kingdoms; he would rule Edmund's
kingdom of Wessex in the south west while the duplicitous Eadric ruled
the central England kingdom of Mercia, which then stretched from the
mouth of the Humber to the mouth of the Avon; Thorkell the Tall, who
had changed sides several times during Aethelred's reign, took charge of
East Anglia. Largely Scandinavian Northumbria continued to be held by
Eric of Norway, who had served Swein as regent in his own land and had
been made earl in Northumbria by Cnut, probably early in 1016 after its
earl, Uhtred, was killed by Cnut. This administrative arrangement may have
displaced a number of earldormen, or at least put their noses out of joint,
but it was not to last long.

Eadric, who clearly had not appreciated that Cnut was not Aethelred,
was the first to go. Within a few months he was doubtless once more up to
the usual tricks which he had got away with for so many years, but either
suspected or found to be treasonous, he was quickly killed without even
the semblance of a trial. According to William of Malmesbury, 'the traitor
was strangled in the chamber where they (he and Cnut) sat, and thrown
out of the window into the River Thames, thus meeting the just reward of
his perfidy'. The *Encomium* to Emma improbably named the executioner
as Eric, earl of Northumbria, and claimed Eadric was despatched with a
Viking axe.[5] Neither source was shedding any tears for Eadric. Thorkell
remained Cnut's closest adviser for four years, and probably acted as regent
in Cnut's absence from England in 1019-20, but in November 1021 he was
dramatically outlawed for some unknown cause and fled from England,
never to return. Cnut's biographer suggested Thorkell may have been
seeking to exploit to his own advantage resentment of Danish rule in his
earldom of East Anglia, which had suffered repeatedly and badly in Danish
raids.[6] Eric was also said by the near-contemporary English historians to

have fled from Cnut's wrath, though Norse sources suggested he had died in England in 1023, from loss of blood after an operation,[7] which is perhaps more likely, given that his loyalty to Swein and then to his son was never questioned. Regional government then reverted to the rule of a mixture of some Danish but mainly Anglo-Saxon earldormen. Thus England seems to have remained largely Anglo-Saxon in nature despite Danish rule.

Within a short time Cnut had quashed any immediate threat to his rule and made provision for the administration of the realm. 'Everything having been thus duly settled,' said the *Encomium* to Emma, 'the king lacked nothing except a most noble wife'. There followed an implausible Cinderella-type story in which Cnut ordered 'such a one ... to be sought everywhere for him ... Therefore journeys were undertaken throughout realms and cities and a royal bride was sought; but it was with difficulty that a worthy one was found, after being sought far and wide.' She was, said the encomiast, 'a lady of the greatest nobility and wealth, but yet the most distinguished of the women of her time for delightful beauty and wisdom, inasmuch as she was a famous queen. In view of her distinguished qualities of this kind, she was much desired by the king, and especially because she derived her origin from a victorious people, who had appropriated for themselves part of Gaul, in despite of the French and their prince.' Now who could that be? 'Why should I make a long story of this?' added the encomiast, before continuing to do so. 'Wooers were sent to the lady, royal gifts were sent, furthermore precatory messages were sent,' and so on.[8]

The object of Cnut's affections, or at least of his marital intentions, was of course none other than Aethelred's queen, Emma of Normandy, who might well have expected high praise in the *Encomium*, since she was paying for it. Whether she was in fact the vision of loveliness and womanly virtues depicted by the encomiast is unknown, but certainly the tables were now turned, and the former teenage bride must have been at least 30 years old with three children, while her putative bridegroom, who appeared in a contemporary illustration as tall, handsome and bearded, was probably a lad of no more than 17 or 18 years old; certainly he cannot have been much more than 20. However, it would become clear that Cnut had something more in mind than romance when he sent for Emma.

Why was Cnut so intent on contracting this marriage? William of Malmesbury suggested there were two reasons: '... so that while they [the Anglo-Saxons] were paying obedience to their accustomed sovereign, they should the less repine the dominion of the Danes. Another design was to acquire favour with Richard [of Normandy], who would think little of his nephews so long as he supposed he might have others by Cnut.' Forced marriage by carrying off the widow of your enemy was common in Scandinavia – thus Cnut's father Swein had married the widow of king

Eric of Sweden – and could have made a point to the English before Edmund's death, but the former reason, Emma's familiarity to the English as queen, though it might have been a useful by-product of the match, was probably not so important in 1017. In the immediate aftermath of Cnut's accession, keeping the English happy was probably not particularly high on his agenda, and it has to be wondered what Emma's stock might be with the English after, like Hamlet's mother, she hastened to the marriage bed of the man who had so viciously assailed her late husband. It was most likely relations with Normandy which preoccupied Cnut. Even though his rule was encountering no serious opposition in England, he apparently still feared potential rivals abroad, not least Edward and Alfred, the sons of Aethelred, who had a far better claim to the throne than he did, which might conceivably have been supported morally by the pope and militarily by the duchy. To forestall any such action, Cnut needed to conclude an alliance with the duchy, and as with Aethelred 15 years earlier, a royal marriage would be the key to that. Emma was a valuable diplomatic bargaining counter.

The *Encomium* does at least give an apparently realistic account of the marriage negotiations, which probably took place with Richard of Normandy, as was the custom, though Emma is likely to have had considerable influence over them. The account made clear that it was not the position of her children by Aethelred which concerned Emma: 'For she had information that the king had had sons by some other woman'.[9] That woman was Aelfgifu of Northampton, daughter of Aelfhelm, former earl of Northumbria and a major landowner in Northamptonshire. According to thirteenth-century Danish historian Saxo Grammaticus,[10] she was previously the mistress of Olaf the Stout, that same Olaf Haroldson who had fought for Aethelred and subsequently became king of Norway, but Cnut stole her away to be his mistress. She may have been older than Cnut, but she was probably younger than Emma. She bore him two sons: Swein, perhaps named after his father, and Harald, perhaps after his older brother or his grandfather, and the *Encomium* suggested that they had already been born in 1017, which implied that the liaison with Aelfgifu was at least two years old. She was a 'handfast' or temporary wife and he never married her, but despite the undoubted disapproval of the church, he never abandoned her; in fact Stenton suggested[11] that he encouraged her to act as his queen in the north of England, where she probably remained, well away from court, and there is charter evidence which implies that she had considerable status there.

There is some controversy about where Emma was at the time of the marriage negotiations, which could have had a significant effect on how they were conducted. Neither the chronicles nor the near-contemporary historians have anything to say on this subject, simply indicating that Cnut had her brought to him to be his queen. This unaccustomed silence may mean that they didn't know where she was at the time, or that they didn't think it important enough to mention, but it has allowed one of Emma's recent biographers to claim that she had returned from Normandy to London, where she remained throughout 1016 and became a prisoner of the Danes.[12] In this version, she was forced to marry Cnut as a symbol of the submission of England to Viking domination, but though Emma may well have returned to support the fight against the Danes, it seems unlikely that she would have stayed on in England after Ashingdon, or after she became a widow and a son of Aethelred's first marriage began his fight for the succession. After reviewing what little evidence there is, Alistair Campbell, translator of the *Encomium*, was convinced that she was in Normandy at the time.[13] Even if she had stayed to be near her substantial English landholdings, Cnut would have been a fool to try to force her into marriage and incur the enmity of her brother in Normandy.

The *Encomium*[14] seemed to suggest that the marriage negotiations took place at a distance, which might imply Normandy, and even given the exaggeration of that work, Emma appeared to be very much in control and setting conditions under which she would be prepared to marry, while Cnut was depicted as suing for the match. Her chief condition of course related to Aelfgifu. To ensure the marriage went ahead, Cnut had to take a solemn oath to Emma that 'he would never set up the son of any wife other than herself to rule after him, if it happened that God should give her a son by him'. Thus Emma hoped she had ensured that the sons of Aelfgifu would not succeed to the throne in England, though not, as it turned out, in other dominions that Cnut acquired, which no-one in Normandy had apparently thought to ask him to swear to, and even in England the situation was to prove more complex than she had hoped.

By July of 1017 Cnut and Emma were married and, said the *Encomium*, 'the English rejoiced',[15] though translator Alistair Campbell was not so sure:

> … we may doubt that the English regarded Emma with sufficient affection to feel any enthusiasm for her astonishing recovery of her former position in 1017, much less to change their feelings towards their conqueror on her account, but she evidently wished it to be thought that they did so, and instructed her Encomiast accordingly.[16]

The description of the 'magnitude of delight'[17] which arose in the 'happy couple' also seems exaggerated with Aelfgifu in the background, though perhaps there might be some truth to this in Emma's case. Her handsome, young husband must have been a striking contrast as a lover to the ageing Aethelred, and her later championing of the Danish cause, even in opposition

2 A monastic illustration from a contemporary manuscript, of King Cnut and Queen Emma presenting an altar cross to New Minster, Winchester, where both were eventually to be buried. *Copyright British Library Board MS Stowe 944 f6r.*

to the cause of her sons by Aethelred, suggested a strong attachment; perhaps Emma had finally made a love match. The question now was, could Emma give Cnut a son and heir? That question was answered in the affirmative soon afterwards and the child was named Harthacnut, combining his father's name with a prefix meaning swift or strong. The parents, said the *Encomium*, were profoundly happy. They also had a daughter, Gunnhild, who was perhaps named after Cnut's aunt who was executed on Aethelred's orders in the St Brice's day massacre. Had Emma proved childless, Edward and Alfred, her sons by Aethelred, would have continued to have a valid claim to the throne of England, albeit with no means of enforcing it, but when their mother gave birth to Harthacnut they were effectively disinherited, and now seemed condemned to permanent landless exile in Normandy.

In 1018 Cnut embarked on what, in modern political terms, we would call a 'charm offensive'. In late spring or early summer he despatched most of his army back to Scandinavia with the Danegeld he had collected for them, retaining only 40 ships with him – a graphic demonstration of his intention to rule by consent of the English not by the force of an army of occupation. It must also have been welcome relief to those Englishmen who feared more massive collections of tribute while the army stayed. He then, said William of Malmesbury, 'began to conciliate the English with unceasing diligence; allowing them equal rights with the Danes in their assemblies, councils and armies'. Cnut held a national council at Oxford which was attended by Englishmen and Danes from across the country, at which it was agreed that all would abide by 'Edgar's law', the legal code of the much-respected tenth-century king. This was an important departure because the 'Danelaw' had traditionally been an area in which the law of the conquerors had been paramount; now all were to be subject to one unified code of English law.

Despite the ruthlessness of the start of his reign, Cnut, like Hrolfr in Rouen, quickly appreciated the importance to his cause of the church, which had suffered heavily from Danish depredation; ecclesiastical historian Orderic Vitalis said 'cathedrals and monasteries with all their books and treasures were destroyed'.[18] Cnut set about repairing the damage – to relations and buildings – of the years prior to his accession. All contemporary sources indicate that he embraced Christianity with some enthusiasm, though his love life had shown that he could be somewhat selective in which of its precepts he would honour in the observance. In this he was following the example of his father, Swein Forkbeard, who at one time was said to have persecuted Christians, but had latterly become at least a nominal Christian and discouraged worship of the old Scandinavian gods in Norway, and had also given land to a Christian bishop performing missionary work in Norway and Sweden. Early in his reign Cnut began the work of restoring those monasteries which he and his father had left ruinous after the years of raiding, and many of them subsequently received valuable gifts from the king. He also set about building churches at the places where he had fought in his campaign for the crown, especially Ashingdon where Edmund was finally defeated, and 'appointed ministers to them, who through succeeding ages might pray to God for the souls of the persons there slain'. Cnut was present at the consecration of Ashingdon together with all the nobles of England, and he gave to the church his own priest, Stigand, though Cnut's dedication did not long outlast him; by William of Malmesbury's time Ashingdon had become an ordinary parish church. There is still a church on the site at Ashingdon today, and the south wall at the east end is said to survive from Cnut's original building.

Mindful of the story of his father's death, Cnut also built, or rather re-built, a church of 'princely magnificence ... over the body of the most holy

Edmund, whom the Danes of former times had killed'. A monastery at what was then known as Beadarichesworth had originally been built by Sigeberht, the seventh-century king of East Anglia, who later abdicated and became a monk there. The church and monastery were renamed Edmundsburh after Edmund's relics were deposited there, only becoming Bury St Edmunds in later centuries. In 1020 Cnut refounded the monastery as an impressive Benedictine abbey. More than 500ft long, with a west front more than 250ft wide, it was one of the greatest churches in England. In the twelfth century William of Malmesbury said it still 'surpasses almost all the monasteries of England'. Only a fragment of the original building survives today.

The *Encomium* to Emma gushes over Cnut's visits to the restored holy sites: 'When he had entered the monasteries … he advanced humbly, and with complete concentration prayed for the intercession of the saints in a manner wonderfully reverent, fixing his eyes upon the ground, and freely pouring forth … rivers of tears'.[19] An act which must have gained much credit amongst churchmen was the return, six years after Cnut's accession, of the remains of Archbishop Alfheah, murdered by Thorkell the Tall's men, from London back to Canterbury, in which Emma took an important part.

This affection for religion had its advantages for Cnut, something such an accomplished politician will have been quick to appreciate. The church was the only source of legitimacy for an eleventh-century king, and Cnut needed its seal of approval as 'the Lord's anointed' to consolidate his legitimacy in England, and increase his power in northern Europe. Despite this, there is evidence of Cnut commissioning a decorative frieze for the Old Minster in Winchester, capital of the kingdom of Wessex, depicting an heroic tale from ancient Skaldic poetry rooted in Scandinavia's pagan past, but this was his culture and there is no reason to suppose that he saw it as conflicting with his Christian beliefs; in fact his modern biographer said 'he became extravagantly pious'.[20] He was not alone amongst kings of England in employing skaldic poets who would write paons of praise to their warrior prowess, whether justified or not. The revered Edgar, father of both Aethelred and his murdered half-brother Edward, who brought peace and prosperity to a unified England between 959 and 975, probably invited skaldic poets into the country, and Aethelred apparently followed his example, patronising a skald named Gunnlaug Serpent-tongue.

Cnut's Christian belief was seen nowhere better than in his remarkable letter of 1020 to the people of England, which showed that he had achieved his goal of respectability as a ruler through relations with the church, since it referred to letters and messages to him brought from the pope in Rome personally by Archbishop Lyfing, whom Cnut had doubtless despatched there as his ambassador. In part the letter, which is of some 600 or 700 words in length, gives news of a recent expedition to Denmark and emphasises the king's strenuous efforts to ensure the security of his subjects, but much of it is taken up with exhortations to religious duty and observance in daily life by all classes of society, and shows clearly how this was intended to support the legitimacy of Cnut's regime:

> Now I pray my archbishops and all my diocesan bishops, that they all may be zealous about God's dues, each in the district which is entrusted to him; and also I charge all my earldormen that they help the bishops in furthering God's rights and my royal dignity and the benefit of all the people.
>
> If anyone, ecclesiastic or layman, Dane or Englishman, is so presumptuous as to defy God's law and my royal authority or the secular law, and he will not make amends and desist according to the directions of my bishops, I then pray, and also command, Earl Thorkell, if he can, to cause the evil-doer to do right.[21]

The letter was probably drafted or advised on by Archbishop Lyfing, but Cnut does not appear to be a man likely to allow the dissemination in his name of sentiments with which he disagreed, so we must allow that it represented his heartfelt views. Since no-one outside the clergy would have been able to read this letter, it was probably disseminated through the churches and read to congregations. Thus Archbishop Lyfing cemented the young Dane's claim to the throne of England, but the lengthy and hazardous trip to Rome must have been too much for the elderly holy man and he died soon afterwards.

Henry of Huntingdon confirmed the embassy to Rome, but wrongly claimed that it was the task of Lyfing's successor, Aethelnoth, probably due to some confusion in dating in the Worcester chronicle, and the fact that Aethelnoth did visit Rome in 1022 to be confirmed in his post, as archbishops were then required to do. The confusion is perhaps understandable because there is no mention of Lyfing's embassy in the chronicles, but the letter names him and clearly suggests that he brought the pope's communications from Rome himself. To add to the confusion, there was also another Lyfing, an abbot and subsequent bishop of Crediton, who accompanied Cnut on a highly successful pilgrimage to Rome, probably in 1027, after which Cnut again wrote a letter to the English people which, unlike the earlier letter, is quoted in full by John of Worcester. Henry of Huntingdon enthused of the Rome trip: 'Who may number his alms, his bountiful gifts, and the mighty deeds that the great king performed on the pilgrimage? There was no king within the bounds of the western world who visited the holy places of Rome in so much splendour and glory.' It must have been at this time that Cnut began negotiations for the marriage of Gunnhild, his daughter by Emma, to Henry III of Germany – a diplomatic feat which had never before been achieved by any Scandinavian ruler.

It was Cnut's devotion to religion which apparently gave rise to the most famous anecdote about him. Henry of Huntingdon, presumably relying on oral sources since there was nothing of this in the chronicles, told a story of Cnut trying to turn back the waves, which was corrupted in past school histories into a tale of ultimate folly. In fact, according to Henry, it was never Cnut's intention to turn back the waves, but to demonstrate to his sycophantic courtiers that he had no power to do so. The story developed somewhat through various versions of Henry's manuscript, suggesting embellishment over time, and it may actually have been lifted wholesale from a classical source, since Herodotus had a story of the Persian king Xerxes having the sea flogged for daring to disobey his orders, but the transposition of the moral suggested that it was based on something Cnut actually said or did, or at the very least, on his accepted attitudes and beliefs. The story is not very long and is given below in full:

> … when he was at the height of his ascendancy, he ordered his chair to be placed on the sea-shore as the tide was coming in. Then he said to the rising tide, 'You are subject to me, as the land on which I am sitting is mine, and no-one has resisted my overlordship with impunity. I command you, therefore, not to rise on to my land, nor to presume to wet the clothes or limbs of your master. But the sea came up as usual, and disrespectfully drenched the king's feet and shins. So jumping back, the king cried, 'Let all the world know that the power of kings is empty and worthless, and there is no king worthy of the name save Him by whose will heaven, earth and sea obey eternal laws.' Thereafter King Cnut never wore the golden crown, but placed it on the image of the crucified Lord, in eternal praise of God the great king.

The story probably dated from later in Cnut's reign since he comes across as a man clearly confident in his control of the realm: 'at the height of his ascendancy,' the story said. The anecdote may portray a devout man, but also an intelligent and impatient man who did not suffer fools gladly. It clearly suggested a man who may have looked to heaven but who had his feet firmly on the ground. Perhaps, as Sir Frank Stenton suggested,[22] Cnut's association with the church showed him a new world, beyond anything which existed in Scandinavia at that time – a world of learning and venerable institutions, a world of rights of kingship which extended beyond the power of the sword.

Cnut had every reason to be confident in his later years, since England was to be only the first of the realms he was to rule, and it is not surprising that he is known in Scandinavian history as 'Cnut the Great'. He left England in pursuit of power in Scandinavia as early as 1019, and in the following nine years led at least four expeditions to the region. The first of these was to secure his succession in Denmark following the death of his brother Harald, and no doubt it also forestalled further raids on England from that country, as he suggested in his letter of 1020. Cnut took with him in 1019 both Danish and English troops, and it was in this campaign that we first hear of a man who, albeit inadvertently, probably did as much as anyone to bring about the building of England's first castle.

Cnut stayed in Denmark until the spring of 1020, and though there is no clear indication of any fighting with rival claimants to the throne he did campaign against the Wends, a Slavic people from the southern shores of the Baltic, in what is now northern Germany, who had perhaps taken the opportunity after the death of Harald to push north into Denmark. The story of the campaign against the Wends was told only by Henry of Huntingdon, but William of Malmesbury had a less detailed account of a similar story set during a later campaign in Norway, which suggested that both of them found this story in oral tradition, though memories had faded somewhat as to exactly when it took place. According to Henry, Cnut's army had encamped close to the enemy, intending to attack the next morning, but the English commander decided to launch a surprise night attack and slaughtered and routed the Wends. At dawn Cnut saw that the English had gone and thought they had fled from the battle, but when he advanced on the enemy camp he found only corpses. 'Because of this,' said Henry, 'he henceforth esteemed the English as highly as the Danes'.

The man commanding the English in Henry's story was Godwine, son of Wulfnoth, the Sussex thegn who had taken to piracy and helped destroy Aethelred's fleet in the summer of 1008, after being accused of treason by Eadric's brother. Godwine is not only significant in the story of England's first castle, but in the wider history of England in the first half of the eleventh century. He was to become the most powerful man in the land and create a dynasty probably more powerful than any seen in Anglo-Saxon England. According to the *Vita Eadwardi Regis* ('The Life of King Edward'), another 'written to order' work, this time commissioned by Godwine's daughter Edith, Cnut had summoned Godwine to his side from an early stage in his reign, because 'among the new nobles of the conquered kingdom' he 'was judged by the king himself the most cautious in counsel and the most active in war',[23] perhaps forgetting that the chronicle made clear Thorkell was closest to Cnut prior to his exile in 1021.

William of Malmesbury claimed Godwine received his earldom for his courage in the engagement, suggesting he was previously perhaps only a thegn, as his father had been. William's version was based on a 'rags to riches' story of Godwine's antecedents, apparently derived from tales invented by skalds after his rise to power, in which he was depicted as a farmer or cowherder's son who began his rise by coming to the assistance of an earl lost after a battle, or even of Aethelred, lost while out hunting. It certainly gives the impression that Anglo-Saxon England, unlike stratified Norman society, was a place where a man might, potentially at least, rise from humble beginnings by his own efforts, though the relative mobility or otherwise of Anglo-Saxon and Norman societies has long been hotly contested by historians and any brief summary is likely to be disputed by some academic or other.

Pre-Conquest English society might outwardly seem relatively static. The broad mass of the population were serfs, whence we get the word 'servile', and perhaps also 'service'; they were effectively slaves tied to a lord, with nothing to speak of in the way of legal rights. All above them had rights and duties defined by law. Their immediate superiors were the ceorls or peasant farmers, free men farming their own land who, in some cases, were even free to chose their own lord, and could thus afford far greater freedom of expression towards the lord, hence the word 'churlish'. Nobility was, superficially at least, simpler than that of Norman-ruled England. There were no dukes or knights in Anglo-Saxon England, only earls or earldormen, and thegns. Though to confuse matters further, earls might style themselves *dux* or duke and thegns witnessed charters with the title of 'minister' or armed retainer, a knight by another name. These titles were also changing during the eleventh century. Danish influence was simplifying the Anglo-Saxon earldorman to earl, an Anglicization of the Scandinavian *jarl*, and Housecarl, or *huskarl* in old Danish, was the Scandinavian equivalent of thegn, which came to be applied to personal military retainers like the men who so courageously supported Harold at Hastings.

If the earls were the great and the powerful, the thegns were the backbone of English government and society, and achieving the lower level of that status was not beyond the reach of an industrious and ambitious farmer. Though customs may have varied, at some times and in some parts of the country, a ceorl who possessed five hides of land – a hide was the measure of land notionally needed to support a household – was well on his way to thegnly status. A merchant could qualify with three crossings of the open sea at his own expense. A thegn might control the whole of an old kingdom or just a shire or two. The most powerful might be very little less important than earls, while the least so might serve another more powerful thegn and have little more power than the average ceorl.

Godwine becoming a thegn through good fortune, and winning his earldom on the field of battle could therefore be feasible, but unfortunately here the facts seem to spoil a good story, because there is evidence that Godwine witnessed a land charter as an earldorman in 1018,[24] the year before

Cnut's first foreign expedition. There may, therefore, be some truth in the *Vita*'s claim that Cnut identified Godwine as useful at an early stage, perhaps because of his control of the Sussex ports, though interestingly it also offers, without details, the claim that he received his earldom after one of Cnut's foreign expeditions. This perhaps suggests that Edith, Godwine's daughter, had little knowledge of her father's early career and the anonymous writer of the work filled in the gaps with the tall tales of the skalds, though it was entirely possible that Godwine, already an earl, was given a greater earldom to reward his success in battle. One of Godwine's biographers suggested that he may have been given an earldormanry in central Wessex as early as 1016, after the death of the holder at Ashingdon,[25] and the family's other biographer is convinced that Godwine was of royal blood, a descendant of Aethelwulf, the king of the West Saxons until his death in 858, who traced his descent from Cerdic, the mythical sixth-century founder of the dynasty.[26]

What is certain is that Cnut was a warrior prince, unlikely to far advance any man who had not proved himself in battle, so the young earldorman's decisive intervention during a foreign expedition, whenever it took place, may have been the true start of Godwine's rise. Certainly Godwine, like his father, was never accused of lacking daring and physical courage, though he was to be accused of many other things during the next few decades.

Chapter Three

The Rise of Godwine

In the course of Cnut's 20-year reign England was to become just a part, albeit a wealthy part, of a great northern empire which included Norway and Denmark, created by the young king's ambition and restless energy. Perhaps after the years of Viking raiding, the daily round of kingship was simply too tedious. Whatever the reason, the expedition to Denmark in 1019-20 was just the start of a series of northern expeditions; adventurous exploits which added to Cnut's legendary reputation in Scandinavia.

In 1022 the *Chronicle* said he gathered his ships, apparently at the Isle of Wight, though no-one seemed to know why, since Wight was the rallying point for France; Sandwich was a more suitable rally point for a northern expedition. It was not until his return in the following year that the reason for the secrecy and subterfuge became clear. Cnut had launched a daring expedition to Denmark to confront Thorkell the Tall, who had established a worryingly strong power base there since his return to the country on exile from England in 1021. Whether Cnut intended a pitched battle to decide the issue is not known, but doubtless Thorkell could muster considerable forces, and a settlement, probably proposed by Thorkell, was agreed and the two former Viking raiders were reconciled, at least in principle. They guaranteed the settlement in the traditional manner, with an exchange of hostages, in this case their sons. Thus Cnut's son, the young Harthacnut, aged only four or five, and Cnut's kingdom of Denmark, passed into the safekeeping of Thorkell, the man who had betrayed his father in 1012, and whose actions as regent in England had caused Cnut to exile him in 1021.

If Cnut was uneasy about this settlement, worse was to come. Within three years Thorkell was dead, apparently of natural causes, and Cnut appointed as regent the Danish earl Ulf, husband of Cnut's sister Estrith, who also became guardian of Harthacnut. But trouble was brewing in the region. Denmark now had the backing of the vast wealth of England and this had disturbed the delicate balance of power in Scandinavia. In 1026

Olaf Haroldson, ruler of Norway, whose mistress, Aelfgifu, Cnut had stolen, allied himself with King Anund of Sweden, apparently with the intention of raiding Scania, the richest of the Danish provinces, in the extreme south of modern-day Sweden. For some unaccountable reason, Ulf, Cnut's Danish regent, and his brother Eilaf, whom Cnut had made an earl in England, decided to join this coalition; perhaps the brothers hoped to win Denmark for themselves and drive Cnut out.

Predictably, Cnut launched a daring attack which initially took his enemies by surprise. Olaf was still at sea, off the island of Sjaelland, east of Denmark, when Cnut attacked with a larger force, driving Olaf's fleet east towards the Baltic in confusion. Cnut had begun well and no doubt had every expectation of success when he met the Swedish ships at the mouth of the Holy river in the east of Scania, but at that point his campaign began to unravel. A Scandinavian source said Olaf had dammed the river, and when he released the dam many of Cnut's ships were overwhelmed. Another source said Ulf lured many of the men from Cnut's force who managed to make it on shore to their deaths, by offering them battle at a location which could only be reached across a decrepit bridge. Many of the facts are difficult to pin down, but there is no reason to doubt the *Chronicle's* report that there was great loss of life amongst Cnut's men, nor to doubt that at the Holy River he suffered his most resounding defeat. Northern tradition said that Cnut's revenge on the earl who had betrayed him was not long in coming: Ulf was murdered soon afterwards.[1]

Cnut had no intention of allowing this defeat to stand, but it was his subtlety more than his strength in battle which was finally to win the day. During the following two years Cnut looked for Olaf's weak points and began to exploit them ruthlessly. He quickly found it was not hard to discover disaffected noblemen in Olaf's Norway. Olaf ruled as an autocrat and, worse still for the 'heathen' Norwegians, he was a Christian autocrat, ruthlessly determined to root out worship of the old Norse gods. Cnut began to seduce the Norwegian nobility with bribes and promises of advancement if they supported his claim to Olaf's throne. As a result, he defeated Olaf without fighting a single battle. He was prepared for battle, setting out from England in 1028 with fifty ships, augmented by another fleet from Jutland, but Olaf's support had dwindled away to such an extent that he dared not offer battle, and Cnut's process up the Norwegian coast turned into a triumphal progress, with acclamation of his rule when he landed at Nidaros. Olaf went into exile within a few months, but the old warrior could not simply fade away; in the following year he raised a small army in Sweden in the forlorn hope of regaining his throne, but fell in the attempt.

With Scotland also submitting to Cnut, his power had now reached its zenith. He was indisputable ruler of a northern empire unmatched in

Europe, controlling the most dangerous part of the vital trade route from the Bay of Biscay to the eastern Baltic – but the continued existence of this empire would depend on his sons. Cnut immediately held a great court at Nidaros, now Trondheim, at which he proclaimed Harthacnut, his son by Emma, king of Denmark, though the boy cannot then have been older than 10. In Norway he decided to appoint a regent with the title of earl, and was politically astute enough to give the honour to the popular but ineffective Hakon, son of the late earl Eric, who had formerly ruled Norway in that capacity for Swein Forkbeard, and was appointed earl of Northumbria by Cnut in 1016. On Hakon's death at sea less than a year later, Cnut appointed Swein, one of his sons by Aelfgifu, to rule Norway under his mother's guardianship – and in subjection to Emma's son in Denmark. It was a disastrous decision.

Aelfgifu's rule made Olaf's despotism seem benign by comparison; so much so that Olaf's adherence to Christianity quickly led to a cult of Saint Olaf in Norway, which even spread to England, with churches in London, York, Exeter and elsewhere dedicated to St Olave. The problem was not just Aelfgifu's autocratic manner, but her imposition of Danish-style taxation, heavier public service and increased penalties for violence on what Sir Frank Stenton called 'the most fiercely independent people in Europe'.[2] The cult of St Olaf led to a resurgence of national feeling and revulsion against Danish rule in Norway, and in the autumn of 1035 the old warrior achieved in death what he had failed to do in life, when Aelfgifu and Swein were finally forced to flee to Denmark, and Olaf's son Magnus was acclaimed king of Norway.

What of Godwine, the man whose actions in an earlier expedition so impressed Cnut, and whose actions in the crisis of 1051 may have led directly to the building of England's first castle? It is possible that he accompanied Cnut on several of his voyages of conquest, though there is no further mention of him in this respect. Certainly he quickly became a trusted lieutenant to the Dane after Thorkell was exiled, though exactly when and how is as much a mystery as many other aspects of his early life.

Godwine was probably born about 993[3] of a Saxon family which would have been amongst those bearing the brunt of the Viking raids, and the inevitable compromises made by those determined to survive those troubled times may be the cause of the conspicuous and curious silence on this period in the *Vita*, which after all is intended to chronicle his family's deeds. Frank Barlow, modern biographer of Godwine's family,[4] suggested that Godwine's father, Wulfnoth, thegn of the South Saxons (Sussex), was punished by Aethelred for his piracy by confiscation of his considerable estates, and that Godwine's grandfather, Aethelmaer, earl of western Wessex, also suffered confiscation as punishment for surrendering to Swein Forkbeard in 1013, though he was hardly alone in that. According to Aethelred's biographer,[5] Aethelmaer held his earldom until about 1015, when he probably died, but he may have had lands confiscated and it certainly seems that some of Wulfnoth's estates were taken.

There may also have been other skeletons in the family cupboard. Though the *Encomium* to Emma insisted that Cnut favoured those who had served Edmund 'faithfully without deceit',[6] his promotion of the duplicitous Eadric Streona clearly showed that this policy was simply for 'public consumption', and it is questionable to what extent Godwine was faithful to the luckless Edmund during the course of that troubled year 1016. In the circumstances it is perhaps hardly surprising that the commissioned author of the *Vita* chose not to dwell on Godwine's early years. What was clear, then as later, was that Godwine could lead a charmed life. In June 1014 – by which time Wulfnoth was dead – Aethelred's eldest son, Aethelstan, was dying and in his will he returned to Godwine an estate at Compton, Sussex, which his father had held; presumably at that time at least Godwine must have been an adherent of the Wessex royal family. Subsequently, as Cnut's faithful servant, he was to acquire massive estates beyond anything which had been held by his father or grandfather.

According to the *Vita* and its translator, it was on the successful conclusion of the 1019 expedition that Cnut promoted Godwine and gave him for his wife his sister-in-law Gytha, the sister of Ulf who had married Cnut's sister Estrith,[7] and daughter of the legendary Thurgils Sprakaleg who, according to a colourful Scandinavian tradition, was reputed to be descended from a bear. Gytha, then probably just a teenager, was said to have given Godwine six sons and three daughters[8] but, like most of the family, controversy was to be attached to her life. On their return home Cnut was said to have appointed Godwine 'office-bearer of almost all the kingdom'. Then or later – there is no certainty of the exact date – Godwine was also created earl of all Wessex, the ancient West Saxon kingdom and the traditional power base of English kings from Alfred onwards. This was the vital region which Cnut had reserved for himself in the administrative shake-up of 1017, but fresh from his success in confirming his control of Denmark, and confident of his control of England, Cnut had no need of such a power base, and clearly wanted this crucial region held by a subordinate whose loyalty to him was unquestionable. Godwine's control of this territory was to prove crucial however in the events leading to the crisis of 1051.

Godwine was not the only 'new man' at Cnut's court. One of them, Leofric, was ennobled as early as 1017. The chroniclers recorded that earldorman Northman was one of three innocent men put to death at the same time as Eadric Streona, perhaps wrongly suspected of involvement in some scheme of Eadric's, and Northman's brother, Leofric, was made earldorman in his place. John of Worcester said Cnut 'afterwards held him in great affection'. His family may have been related to the family of Aelfgifu of Northampton,[9] and he was to be elevated to the earldom of Mercia and become a member of Cnut's elite inner circle of advisers with Godwine, who would be his great rival in the years ahead. Leofric's lady, Godgifu, is well-remembered under the Anglicized name of Godiva, for her legendary naked ride through Coventry market place to persuade her husband to reduce taxes. This story did not first appear until 200 years later, in Roger of Wendover's *Flowers of History*,[10] which may suggest that it was an oral tradition or came from a work later lost.

Some time after Eric of Norway's death in 1023 Cnut appointed Siward, a Dane, to be earl of Northumbria. He does not appear to have been as close to Cnut, perhaps for purely geographical reasons. His nickname was 'the Strong', and a colourful twelfth-century tradition claimed his father had furry ears because he was descended from a white bear and a noblewoman. Henry of Huntingdon described him as 'almost a giant in stature, very strong mentally and physically'; he was, said Stenton, 'a Danish warrior of a primitive type'.[11] Siward was immortalised by Shakespeare in Macbeth as the commander of the English forces which helped to put Malcolm on the throne of Scotland in 1054, but he also seems to have been deprived of his true place in history, since Shakespeare has the tyrant killed by Macduff, while according to John of Fordun, the first Scottish historian writing in the fourteenth century, Macbeth was slain by Siward,[12] or perhaps by his men since he must by then have been a fairly old man. He died the following year.

Godwine was however the chief amongst these nobles. From at least 1023 charter evidence shows that he was second only to Cnut in England, and he may therefore have acted as regent during some of the king's absences from the country, though there are no records. Clear evidence of his pre-eminence was the removal of Worcestershire, Herefordshire and Gloucestershire from Mercia in the early years of Cnut's reign,[13] very likely with encouragement from Godwine. All of these lands were later held by Godwine's family and considerably strengthened him at the expense of his rival, Leofric of Mercia.

What Godwine's relationship with Cnut may have been, other than sovereign and faithful subject, is nowhere recorded directly by the chroniclers and historians, though some clues may be available. Outwardly they both seem from contemporary accounts – albeit accounts from monastic writers with little apparent taste for the delights of secular life – to be surpassingly colourless figures. The *Vita* describes Godwine as a caring and dutiful administrator and father figure to his inferiors, who 'did not discard the gentleness he had learnt from boyhood'.[14] Cnut is described by the historians as an energetic ruler and warrior, but beyond that we are treated only to descriptions of his piety. These are hardly plausible portraits of two young men, both still in their twenties, who had tasted the intoxication of victory in battle and acquired massive wealth and power in a world dominated by violence and conquest. The Godwineist *Vita*[15] said Cnut valued Godwine for his wisdom, courage and eloquence, but there is no doubt that they shared a ruthlessness which was essential for a successful career in power at that time; Godwine was doubtless a subordinate who could always be trusted to enforce the king's will. With so much in common, they may also have shared friendship as young men with other like interests.

Old Norse literature described Cnut as a great and wealthy king who 'attracted potential enemies to his court, overawed them by his splendour, and then disarmed them by bribes,'[16] which seems to be a memory of his corruption of the Norwegian nobility prior to his bloodless triumph there in 1028. Beyond this there seems to be no description of his court. Obviously he liked to impress, and though there are none of the descriptions of drinking and womanising which marked Aethelred's reign, there is no reason to suppose that he was averse to female company; he had, after all, taken Aelfgifu of Northampton as his mistress when he was probably still in his teens. Likewise there is nothing, aside from the nine children his wife bore him, to suggest that Godwine was especially fond of female company, but these were two young men who, though they did not let it affect their ability to wield power, doubtless must have enjoyed lighter moments at court, which may well have included a certain amount of carousing and wenching, and they may have become close as a result.

Whether from fealty or friendship, Godwine apparently named his first sons by Gytha Swein and Harold, to honour Cnut's family, though exactly which members of it were referred to is intriguingly open to question. The boys, the second of whom was the last Anglo-Saxon king of England, may have been named, respectively, after Cnut's father and his brother or grandfather, but Swein and Harold were also the names of Cnut's first two sons, that is, his sons by Aelfgifu of Northampton. If Godwine did indeed name his sons after Aelfgifu's less legitimate offspring, this implied the sort of total commitment to Cnut which disregarded any political danger that might later ensue from seeming to snub Emma. Godwine owed his meteoric rise to Cnut and it would seem he returned this commitment with absolute loyalty. He was Cnut's man and would judge subsequent sovereigns by the standard of the royal Dane he undoubtedly so admired, which was to sow the seeds of conflict when he was confronted, within a few years, with a very different ruler.

On 12 November 1935 Cnut died at Shaftesbury. His death must have been a shock to the country and to those close to him, since he was only about

40 years old and had always been a vigorous and energetic man. Perhaps an old battle wound had finally carried him off, but there is no indication of the cause of his death in the chronicles or histories. At least, unlike Edmund Ironside and many of those who had initially opposed his rule of England, he probably died in his bed. He was buried at the Old Minster at Winchester amidst, according to the *Encomium* to Emma, much national grief: '… all who had heard of his death were moved … The Lady Emma, his queen, mourned together with the natives, poor and rich lamented together, the bishops and clerics wept with the monks and nuns …'.[17] In the 1120s Henry of Huntingdon was to sum up Cnut's reign with these words: 'Before him there had never been in England a king of such great authority'. His 20-year reign had begun with savagery, but Anglo-Saxon society had civilized him and he became a respected statesman and a ruler with a strong grasp of the importance of law and justice. His control of the northern lands, from which Viking raids had formerly been launched, ensured England's security. He had brought the English a much-needed period of peace and stability which enabled commerce and agriculture to thrive, and he had brought England unprecedented diplomatic links with Europe, but his death led to seven years of uncertainty over the succession which was to bring about the total destruction of everything he had created.

There is much conjecture amongst modern historians about what Cnut had intended the fate of his northern empire to be. He had sworn a solemn oath to Emma that her son, Harthacnut, would succeed him, and the encomiast said that when the boy grew up Cnut 'pledged to him the whole realm which was subject to his command'.[18] Certainly Cnut placed the lad in the senior kingship of Denmark, so he must surely have intended him to rule England also, with Swein as king in Norway, subject to his half-brother's sovereignty. It has been suggested that Cnut's unexpected early death may have led to the confusion which followed it,[19] but in fact his plan was already unravelling even before his death. It was just weeks earlier that Swein and Aelfgifu had been forced to flee to Denmark, and the acclamation of Olaf's son Magnus as king of Norway placed a new and urgent threat on Harthacnut's borders. Historian Eric John went further: 'Had he [Cnut] lived very much longer one suspects that his failures in Scandinavia would have affected his power in England, and his reputation as a strong ruler would have suffered.'[20]

The stage was now set for a final showdown between the two women in Cnut's life; a showdown which only one of them could win. Harthacnut, Cnut's one legitimate son, by Emma of Normandy, was held in Denmark by fears of an invasion from Norway. Swein, Aelfgifu's first-born took no further part in politics after his disastrous Norwegian experience, and died the following year, but his brother Harald, Aelfgifu's second son by Cnut, was in England – and keen to rule. The powerful formed themselves into two camps and the war of words quickly became personal. Harald, whose name is always Anglicized by historians as Harold, had acquired the nickname 'Harefoot', perhaps for his speed of movement, but for some he was far too quick in pursuit of the crown. He had not had a high profile in England and it is entirely possible that some were genuinely unaware that he was Cnut's son, but this was firmly denied by the chroniclers, and the *Encomium* to Emma said predictably that it was 'the assertion of very many people'[21] that Aelfgifu had been unable to bear a child and had stolen one from a servant, while other accounts suggested he was really the son of a priest or a cobbler. Nevertheless Harald was the man on the spot.

Godwine backed Harthacnut, melodramatically declaring, according to William of Malmesbury, that he was the 'defender of the fatherless', and he thus supported Emma, who of course wished to wait for Harthacnut, but Leofric, backed by most of the thegns north of the Thames, backed Harald. At a council at Oxford early in 1036 a compromise was reached and Harald was appointed regent, with Emma installed at Winchester to protect Harthacnut's interests. In an act of studied provocation, she had apparently taken the royal treasury with her, but Harald soon reclaimed it. He now began a concerted campaign to win the crown. Summoning Archbishop Aethelnoth, Harald commanded the holy man to hand over the crown and sceptre and consecrate him as king. Aethelnoth, 'a man gifted with high courage and wisdom,'[22] instead placed the crown and sceptre on the high altar, forbade any bishop to touch them and dared Harald to pick up what he had committed to God. 'He, wretched man, did not know what to do or whither to turn,' said the *Encomium*. 'He used threats … and promised gifts … At length, he departed in despair,' unable to move Aethelnoth. The *Encomium* added: 'When the English observed his behaviour they sorrowed'. The Godwineist *Vita*[23] described Harald as 'an arrogant fellow of bad character,' and there were apparently many who might have agreed with this assessment.

Aelfgifu meanwhile was using slightly more subtle methods, inviting all the leading men to a great party and trying to persuade or bribe them to support Harald, though the result was reportedly that they re-doubled their efforts to persuade Harthacnut to leave Denmark. The source of this story was a letter written by a priest named Immo at the emperor's court, where Cnut and Emma's daughter Gunnhild was married to the future emperor Henry III in 1036. Immo's partiality was made clear by his description of Aelfgifu as a 'wretched and wicked step-mother', trying to deprive Harthacnut of the kingdom by fraud,[24] but the story was undoubtedly true and Aelfgifu's efforts were not as ineffective as her enemies would have wished to believe: by the summer of 1036 she was persuading leading earls, including Godwine, to support her son.

It was later in that same year, according to the chroniclers, that an incident took place which would come back to haunt Godwine during the political crisis of 1051. Either one or possibly both of Emma's sons by her first marriage, Alfred and Edward, who had remained in Normandy with apparently little hope of succession, especially when folk remembered the chaos of their father's reign, suddenly came to England. They did so because of a letter urging them to come and claim their inheritance, which appeared to have been written by their mother, though who actually wrote it has been exercising historians ever since. The letter was later reproduced by Emma's encomiast,[25] who claimed it was forged by Harald to lure into his power two rival claimants to the throne, but it is doubtful that they would have been seen as a threat at that time – as long as they remained in Normandy. Historian Simon Keynes, who wrote an introduction to the *Encomium*, believed the letter was genuinely written by Emma,[26] but that her encomiast needed to obscure this in view of the bloody events which it precipitated. Historian Pauline Stafford, who wrote an account of Emma's life, also felt she was the likeliest author of the letter.[27] By this time it must have become clear that Harthacnut was not coming from Denmark, and Alfred and Edward were the only other claimants who could challenge Harald, but Emma's squalid manipulation of her sons by Aethelred in support of her power struggle with Aelfgifu showed a vicious streak of ruthlessness which her encomiast was bound to try to hide.

Whoever wrote the letter, it had its intended effect and Alfred, and possibly Edward also, sailed from Normandy to England. The various accounts are unusually confused but generally agree on when this took place; William of Malmesbury alone dated the event after the death of Harold and before his half-brother could succeed him, but if that were the case Harthacnut's later friendship to Edward seems unlikely. Norman sources confused the issue further by suggesting that Alfred and Edward travelled separately, though why they would choose to do so was unclear, and that Edward was driven off, with Alfred alone landing successfully. John of Worcester tried to make sense of the various English accounts, whose authors should have had a greater knowledge of what happened after the landing, and it seemed clear from these that the brothers came to England together. He said they brought with them 'many' Norman knights, to judge by figures he gave there could have been as many as 1000 Normans, which may have given the unfortunate impression of an intended invasion – though this is perhaps what it was. They may well have landed at Southampton, where Norman sources said Alfred landed, since it would be the most appropriate landing place for Winchester, and John's account said they went first to visit their mother. He added that their presence was resented by all the leading men, which would hardly have been surprising, since no-one wanted to see a return to the bloody chaos of 1013, with Harthacnut mounting a new Danish invasion. If the brothers were hoping to attract support once they landed, they must have quickly realised that their hopes were in vain.

Whether their mother counselled some decisive action to try to seize the crown from the son of her hated rival is not known, but likely. The brothers evidently disagreed on the best course of action, and Edward cautiously remained in Winchester, perhaps because of the obvious lack of support for them, while Alfred, with the main force, rashly hurried towards London, to 'confer' with Harald, said John of Worcester, which would surely have suggested an attempted coup to contemporaries. John said they were stopped at Guildford by Godwine, who had apparently switched sides to Harald after backing the loser at Oxford. Henry of Huntingdon also improbably placed the incident after Harthacnut's reign, but his background to the incident seemed to have the ring of truth, perhaps from oral sources. Henry said Godwine, 'since he was a mighty earl and a ruthless traitor', hoped to marry his daughter to one of Aethelred's sons by Emma, but thought Alfred would not consider her a worthy match, so he convinced the other nobles that Alfred had brought too large a force of Normans with him and would undoubtedly have promised them English lands, making them a threat to all the English nobility. This could be an example of the folklore which subsequently attached to Godwine, especially since his daughter Edith might only have been about six years old at the time, but in other respects it seems a plausible account.

The *Encomium*,[28] a more contemporary but less reliable source, had a version of the story in which some important details differ. For example, it claimed Alfred was travelling alone and was stopped before visiting his mother, though the account seemed confused on other points, since it was suggested that he was heading for London while English accounts agree Emma was at Winchester. Much of this account however seems to be a more detailed version of the story later told by John. The encomiast said Godwine offered Alfred his protection, and presumably therefore his support, and entertained Alfred and his men with food and drink before they bedded down in various billets; only a few men remained with Alfred. Certainly some alcoholic refreshment would have made it easier to overpower a substantial force, and during the night they were treacherously ambushed, disarmed and bound. The *Encomium* blamed 'men leagued with the abominable tyrant Harald', while John put the blame squarely on Godwine, who was no doubt acting as 'enforcer' for Harald, as he had for Cnut.

What followed was a bloodbath. John said some Normans were put in chains and afterwards blinded. Others were tortured by scalping them and cutting off their hands and feet. '… he (Godwine) also ordered many to be sold (as slaves), and he put 600 men to various pitiable deaths.' He did not, however, harm Alfred – at least not personally. The prince was bound and handed over to others, though who exactly is unknown. He was taken by ship to Ely where he was savagely blinded. The *Encomium* had an horrific account of four men holding Alfred down as his eyes were put out. He was then handed over to the monks there, but they could do little. The *Chronicle* confirmed the basic facts and said: 'nor was a more bloody deed done in this land after the Danes came and peace was made here'. This incident must have taken place in late 1036 and Alfred died, apparently from his injuries, on 5 February 1037. John said when Emma heard of this incident she hurriedly sent Edward back to the safety of Normandy, but he undoubtedly never forgot his brother's killing or those he blamed for it.

We can assume this brutal atrocity was carried out on Godwine's orders, though the Godwineist *Vita* subsequently attempted to re-distribute the blame, saying Alfred had acted inadvisedly and his murder was carried out on Harald's orders.[29] The crime was long remembered by many. Twelfth-century historian Orderic Vitalis said its brutality spurred on vengeful Normans at the battle of Hastings, 30 years later, who 'massacred many thousands of English who long before had unjustly murdered the innocent Alfred with his servants'.[30]

In the following year, the Anglo-Saxon magnates, having tired of waiting for Harthacnut, and with Alefgifu's bribes and entreaties no doubt having some effect, Harald was made king of all England in his own right. Emma, now almost 50, was driven out 'without pity at the beginning of winter'. With her brother long dead, and Alfred's blood on her hands because of the letter which had lured him to England, she would have had few friends in Normandy, and she went instead to Flanders, an area corresponding roughly with modern Belgium and north-east France, where the hospitable Count Baldwin welcomed her and maintained her for some years. Harald ruled for almost four and a half years in all, though Sir Frank Stenton believed his mother, Aelfgifu, was the real ruler,[31] as she had been with Swein in Norway, though apparently without the problems that ensued there; perhaps Aelfgifu had learnt her lesson. Harald died in spring 1040 at Oxford, and was buried in the precincts of the abbey at Westminster, giving Westminster Abbey the first of its many royal connections, though in Harold's case it was to be a short-lived connection.

In the intervening period Harthacnut had concluded a treaty with Magnus which stated that whichever died first bequeathed his realm to the survivor. This freed him to leave Denmark and claim the English throne, and he raised an army. But he held off from action, perhaps knowing that Harald was unwell and instead made an extended visit to his mother in Flanders. If he feared some opposition for the succession he need not have worried – the only other likely candidate was Edward, in exile in Normandy, and

William of Malmesbury said he was 'held in contempt by nearly all', from the indolence of his father's reign. In the event, 'Danes and English then uniting in one common sentiment as to the expediency of sending for Harthacnut,' said William, he was invited into England in June 1040, and acclaimed as king. The *Encomium* said 'he was most graciously received by all the inhabitants'.[32]

The *Encomium* said that Emma returned to England from exile with her son, finally victorious through determination, ruthlessness and good fortune, in the battle of Cnut's wives, though at what cost would become clear after Harthacnut's death. What happened to her great rival, Aelfgifu, does not seem to be recorded anywhere, which is odd considering that she had been a major figure in England for more than 20 years. It is very likely that Emma would have wished to see her rival exiled, as she herself had been forced out of England, but the chroniclers do not record it. It may be that she left England with her grandson, Harald's son, Aelfwine, by a lady named, like his mother, Aelfgifu, though she may have taken that name by marriage. Aelfwine was a name typical of the West Saxon royal dynasty and it could be that his mother was a descendant of that dynasty. Aelfwine was reputed to be the founder of the monastery of Sainte-Foi, Conques,[33] which may suggest that he and his grandmother went to Acquitane, whose ruler, William, had enjoyed friendly relations with Cnut.

Harthacnut had not been in England for at least 15 years, since he was a boy, and he had cautiously brought with him 62 ships loaded with Danish troops, presumably in case of opposition to his rule. One of his first acts as king was to raise the payment for these men by levying a tax 'so heavy that scarcely anyone could pay it', said John of Worcester, though it was apparently in line with the levy 'per rowlock' of the Danegeld collected by Cnut, and at around £32,000 was considerably less than half the total amount, due to the smaller number of ships involved. The thegns were usually the tax collectors, but this levy proved so unpopular that Harthacnut had to send out his housecarls to collect it the following year, and Worcester was burnt in May after the two men sent there were murdered by the populace.

Harthacnut took his revenge on his half-brother Harald for usurping his throne, and on those leading magnates who had supported him, including Godwine but not apparently Leofric, by ordering them to London and making them dig up Harald's body and throw it first into a marsh and then into the Thames: whether they were forced to have this done or to do it personally is not clear. The body – William of Malmesbury said just the head, which had been severed on exhumation – was recovered by a fisherman and hastily conveyed to the Danish community in London who buried it in their cemetery, now St Clement Danes, probably in some secrecy, though word obviously leaked out. John of Worcester said Harthacnut also 'burnt with anger because of his brother Alfred's death', for which he blamed Godwine and others, but also no doubt Harald. Why would he be so enraged against a half-brother he might have known over the death of a half-brother he can hardly have known at all? Perhaps because the desertion of Norway by Aelfgifu and Harald's brother Swein delayed his ascent to the English throne for so long, and forced him to barter away descent of the throne of Denmark, but most tellingly, he was likely to have been inculcated with his mother's bitter hatred of her love rival, Aelfgifu, and her children. Godwine gave the king a gift of a magnificently equipped ship, crewed by 80 hand-picked soldiers, to mollify him over his support of Harald, and also over his involvement in the murder of Alfred, which was blamed entirely on Harald. Very little stuck to the Teflon-coated earl.

In the summer of 1041 Edward, Aethelred's surviving son by Emma, came to England, apparently by invitation, and stayed at Harthacnut's court. The reasons behind this are somewhat unclear, but it was an intriguing development. The *Encomium* said Harthacnut had been 'gripped by brotherly love',[34] which obviously hadn't extended to Harald, and had invited Edward to hold the kingdom jointly with him, though what little evidence survives suggests that Edward probably had little influence. Perhaps Harthacnut's invitation was a gesture of friendship to expiate the death of Alfred, or perhaps the king had some inkling that he was not in good health and needed to consider the succession. The most likely explanation was that for some reason Emma did not expect Harthacnut to rule long, and wanted to ensure the succession would go to a son of hers. Whatever the truth, six months later, less than two years after it had begun, Harthacnut's reign dramatically ended.

During the early summer he was attending the wedding in Lambeth of Gytha, the daughter of powerful magnate Osgood Clapa, and a leading Dane named Tofi the Proud. Osgood flourished during Cnut's reign and may have been a Dane, but it has also been suggested he was a member of an ancient family from what is now the East Midlands, though he was exiled in 1046 and never recovered his position. Tofi was apparently much older than his bride and a staller, or royal official, who attended the shire court at Hereford on the king's business, and founded the college of Holy Cross at Waltham, Essex.[35] John of Worcester described the scene:

> Harthacnut, king of the English, merry, in good health, and in great heart, was standing drinking with the bride and certain men when he suddenly crashed to the ground in a wretched fall while drinking.

He had apparently had a stroke, which left him speechless. Perhaps previous strokes, or perhaps his drinking, had provided the motive for summoning

Edward to England. Harthacnut died soon afterwards, on 8 June, 1042. He was buried at the Old Minster in Winchester, beside his father. John of Worcester said that during his reign he 'did nothing worthy of royal power,' though Henry of Huntingdon was kinder, saying: 'He had been honourable by nature and had the benevolence of youth towards his men'.

Cnut's northern empire was now utterly destroyed. First Norway and now Denmark had passed to Olaf Haroldson's son, Magnus. Cnut's two remaining sons were dead in their early twenties – Harthacnut cannot have been older than 24 and Harald 21 – and the sons of Cnut's sister Estrith were barred from rule in Denmark by Harthacnut's treaty with Magnus. In the 26 years since Cnut had taken power, many Anglo-Saxons had begun to think of England as an Anglo-Danish nation, or as William of Malmesbury put it in relation to the citizens of London, 'from long intercourse with these barbarians, [they] had almost entirely adopted their customs'. No doubt this transition was more marked in the leading cities than in the countryside, but Scandinavian influence had long been felt in many areas of England due to past incursions and settlements. The nation was now to suffer the culture shock of rule by a man who was more Norman than English, and whose reign was to lead England into a major crisis, during which the chroniclers would reveal the existence of England's first Norman castle.

Chapter Four

Seeds of Quarrel

After almost 30 years in exile, Edward, the descendant of a long line of West Saxon kings, stretching back to Alfred the Great and beyond to Cerdic, suddenly found himself in the position he must have long despaired of achieving: he was apparently first in line to the throne of England.

It had been a long road for Edward to reach that enviable position. What his life had been like up to that point is largely a matter for speculation, and there has been plenty of that across the centuries, though it does not enlighten us much in respect to Edward's relationship with his father. He was probably born in 1005 and would have been about eight years old when he was forced to flee to Normandy to escape Swein Forkbeard's marauding army. During the whole of his young life up to that point England had been beset by Viking raids and Edward probably saw little of Aethelred. Edward's biographer, Frank Barlow,[1] pointed out that the heroes at the time of the prince's boyhood were the courageous Edmund Ironside and Scandinavian warriors such as Thorkell the Tall and Olaf Haroldson, but Aethelred was unlikely to have been his son's boyhood hero, 'especially as he [Edward] could hardly have avoided hearing criticism of him'. It is likely therefore that Edward's Norman mother, Emma, was the major influence in the early years of the young prince's life, and Norman influence was to persist in his life to come: it is worth remembering that Edward was not only the descendant of a long line of West Saxon kings, but also of Hrolfr, founder of Normandy, through his mother.

After 1013 Edward spent, at most, only two brief periods in England until he returned in the summer of 1041, aged about 36 years old, and even those brief periods are uncertain. The second was late in 1036, when Alfred was murdered, though it is not certain that Edward was present in England at that time. The first is more certain, at least in part. The *Encomium*[2] implied that Edward and Alfred were back in England with their mother at the time of her marriage to Cnut, and were sent back to Normandy after Harthacnut's birth, but the entry is unclear, the princes are not named and are referred to as the 'other legitimate sons' of Cnut and Emma. Edward must have returned to England after 1013, since he witnessed a charter in 1015,[3] and Scandinavian sources suggested he fought alongside Edmund against Cnut, though this seems unlikely since he could only have been 10 or 11 years old at the time, but the continued presence of the princes after Cnut's takeover seems unlikely in view of the Dane's brutal treatment of Edmund's sons and brother, unless they were trapped and unable to get away. Whatever the exact chain of events, it is certain that in April 1016 Edward lost the father who may have become an embarrassment to him anyway, and in 1017 he was parted from his mother also, leaving him effectively an exiled orphan. These events cannot have helped but have a deep and lasting effect on him; his biographer said he 'always behaved like one who had been deprived of love'.[4]

There is a later story that Edward's education was begun at Ely Abbey at an early age, which also suggested that it was intended he would become a monk. It seems extremely unlikely however that Emma, or her brother in Normandy, would have allowed her firstborn and heir to Aethelred's throne, to be put to such a vocation, though undoubtedly it would have suited Aethelred's sons by his first marriage. The education, or at least a sojourn at Ely, may have been real enough, since Ely could have been safely away from the Viking raids, but the supposed monkish vocation was probably later embroidery on the life of the man who would become known to history as 'the Confessor', because of his piety. Certainly after the princes returned to the duchy, Norman sources made clear[5] that Edward and Alfred were educated as nobles in the ducal court, and they would have been educated as knights, as all Norman nobles were. It was evident that the Normans were somewhat taken with the idea of having a couple of potential kings of England in their midst and Edward was encouraged to sign a couple of later charters as 'king',[6] though he was no such thing at that time. The Normans did not however confer lands on the athelings, and neither did the princes embrace the fate of many exiles by seeking their fortune with the sword in foreign lands, so as they grew older they were probably forced into a wandering existence, seeking support as 'poor relatives' at the courts of their mother's many kin in Brittany, Burgundy and Flanders. Later accounts suggested Edward became so devoted to religion that he reputedly took a vow of chastity, of which more later, and for several centuries after his death he would be revered as England's patron saint, though he also developed a taste for the sensual pleasures of hawking and stag hunting. The fact that he was prepared to sign documents as 'king' suggested however that he had not forgotten the dream of succeeding to his father's throne.

So after all his travails, was Edward finally to rule England? Certainly other contenders were thin on the ground. Cnut's sons and Edward's brother were dead, Edmund's sons were long exiled in Hungary, and there was a deafening silence over Aelfwine, Cnut's grandson by Harald, whose name sounds Anglo-Saxon. There were more distant relatives of Cnut in Scandinavia, but even if their claims had been deemed acceptable, they were embroiled in the campaign which Magnus was forced to launch in Denmark to enforce his rights under the treaty with Harthacnut. In the circumstances it seemed that there was really no-one else to compete for the English succession. That did not mean however that Edward's accession was guaranteed. The system of automatic succession by the eldest royal son, which we still have today and which has so often caused civil strife in past centuries, was introduced to this country by the Normans. The Anglo-Saxons had a quite different and arguably better system, under which those of royal blood were styled 'atheling', or 'throne-worthy', but which succeeded would be the decision of the witan, or council of leading figures in the land, lay and cleric. This could mean that the available man succeeded, as did Harald when Harthacnut, undoubtedly the next in line, was detained in Denmark. However it often meant that the most suitable man for the job was chosen, and that everyone agreed to the choice, or kept talking until they did. Thus violent conflicts over the succession were generally avoided, as were totally unsuitable candidates. Had the system of primogeniture been in place, Alfred the Great would not have become king of England in 871, since the next in line were the children of his brother, Aethelred I, but clearly a child could not be chosen to rule at a time of desperate national crisis. So though Edward seemed the only available candidate, he needed the vote of the council, and there was only one man who could assure him of that – the man generally regarded as his brother's murderer.

Since Edward had been living at Harthacnut's court for about six months he must surely have encountered Godwine, though whether they had anything more than a nodding acquaintance is a matter of speculation, and Edward's instinct may have been to avoid a closer relationship because of Alfred's death, but he must quickly have realised that friendly relations with Godwine would be essential in ensuring his succession. If so, then Edward exhibited a characteristic which was to stand him in good stead in the years that followed. Future events were to show that like many an exile, Edward had learnt patience; he had learnt to smile and bide his time. Now more than ever he needed that skill. William of Malmesbury's account of the precursors to the meeting of atheling and power broker suggested a naivety which neither one was likely to possess, but it did also suggest a hesitancy on both sides which could be not far from the truth:

Edward receiving the mournful intelligence of the death of Harthacnut, was lost in uncertainty what to do, or whither to betake himself. While he was revolving many things in his mind, it occurred as the better plan to submit his situation to the opinion of Godwine. To Godwine, therefore he sent messengers, requesting that he might in security have a conference with him. Godwine, though for a long time hesitating and reflecting, at length assented.

Security might well have been Edward's major concern in meeting his brother's killer. He had no choice but to meet with Godwine, but he was entering the lion's den. The astute earl of Wessex might well have plans he knew nothing of, to bring back one of Edmund's sons or find some other candidate, little more than a puppet king whose future loyalty to Godwine would be unquestionable. If the earl had any such plan then Edward's death would be a necessary precursor to it. For his part Godwine also had reason to fear the course of events. It may be that Harthacnut's sudden illness and death had taken him by surprise and that he had no plan, but a powerful feeling that his hard-won position could be under threat. Simon Keynes, in his introduction to the *Encomium*, said Godwine 'was the archetypal 'new noble" who had risen to power under Cnut 'and who would have reason to fear the restoration of the native dynasty'.[7] Change was coming, whatever he did, and it could threaten everything he had won under Cnut and retained under his sons. How he could best exploit this situation to his own ends, was a question on which Godwine must have thought long and hard. But he had to either meet with Edward or allow events to pass him by, which could not be an option for an ambitious and powerful man.

According to William, Edward acted as a supplicant when they met and modestly begged Godwine's assistance to return to exile in Normandy now that his brother was dead. If this was so, then Edward was clearly dissembling and Godwine will have known it, but he may well also have appreciated the political skill of a man who could dissemble so outrageously with a straight face; this could be a man after his own heart. William had Godwine instead urge Edward to stay and embrace the succession, since he was well suited to it by his maturity, his habits of discipline and his appreciation of the miseries of the poor which he will have learnt in his long, landless exile. William paraphrases Godwine setting out his proposition in these terms:

Let him [Edward], then, only promise a firm friendship with himself, undiminished honours for his sons, and a marriage with his daughter, and he who was now shipwrecked almost of life and hope, and imploring the assistance of another, should shortly see himself a king.

Was Edward so 'shipwrecked of life and hope' as William suggests? Certainly he was the only available claimant but he was not the only possible claimant. Whilst waging war to secure Denmark, Magnus of Norway was also threatening to invade England, claiming the throne was his under his treaty with Harthacnut. It appeared that Emma might actually have been supporting that claim rather than Edward's,[8] and a Scandinavian claim could have been welcome to those magnates, like Godwine, who had risen under Cnut and had cause to fear the unknown changes which might ensue from the restoration of the Wessex dynasty. So what made Godwine decide to support Edward? Elsewhere William noted that Edward, 'from the simplicity of his manners' was 'little calculated to govern'. Perhaps Godwine saw in the deceptively mild-mannered Edward a monarch he might control, and that certainly seemed to be Godwine's approach in the years that followed. It is not clear where William's account of this meeting comes from. It is not in the chronicles, nor is it in the *Vita* whose writer, presumably following a version of the Abingdon *Chronicle*, seemed not to know that Edward had been in the country for six months and suggested he was fetched from Normandy.[9] This leaves either an earlier source now lost, or an oral tradition, unless we accept that this is literary embroidery, but there is nothing about the account which is entirely implausible. Undoubtedly a meeting must have taken place at some point, at which the two men began to perceive each other's strengths and weaknesses. It is unlikely that Godwine would have spoken so strongly for Edward unless such a meeting had taken place. Whether Godwine would have declared all his purposes so openly as they are expressed in the above quotation is questionable, but there was undoubtedly a price to be paid for his support, of which Edward would become only too aware as his reign progressed, though at this point 'there was nothing which Edward would not promise' to achieve Godwine's support.

There are historians who wish to discredit these accounts and argue that Edward in fact owed no particular debt to Godwine, and that to suggest otherwise is to be duped by a massive conspiracy involving chroniclers and historians over several centuries. Certainly there was considerable folklore which attached to Godwine, during his lifetime and after his death, and a great deal of anti-Godwine propaganda after 1066, designed to discredit Harold Godwineson's claim to the throne and justify William's invasion and conquest, which means that these accounts cannot simply be taken at face value, but then nor can historical accounts from any source or from any period. To assume, because of this, that almost everything written about Godwine must therefore be false seems somewhat disingenuous, and to suggest that the support of the most wealthy and powerful man in the kingdom would be an irrelevance to an atheling with no wealth, friends or power base seems simply naive. A wide range of sources from this period, and the events of the following nine years, strongly suggest that both Edward and Godwine accepted a political deal had been made, and Godwine was owed favours which he spent the next few years calling in.

3 This *c.* 1850 portrait of Edward the Confessor was based on the only contemporary images of him which exist, on coins.

An assembly was convened, either at Gillingham or London, possibly even before Harthacnut had been buried, and Edward was chosen as king, 'as was his natural right' said the *Chronicle*, though it was by no means the foregone conclusion that it might appear to be. John of Worcester recorded that it was 'mainly by the exertions of Earl Godwine and Lyfing, Bishop of Worcester', that the decision was in Edward's favour. William of Malmesbury referred to Godwine's eloquence in support of Edward. Where that failed, 'some were influenced by presents', and those who still resisted 'were carefully marked, and afterwards driven out of England'. So the man whose claim to the throne, just two years earlier, was, according to William, 'held in contempt by nearly all' from the indolence of his father's reign, was now England's chosen king. He was crowned on 3 April 1043 and the *Vita* states: 'Everywhere he was acclaimed with loyal undertakings of submission and obedience'.[10]

Though Edward had an English name and an English father, he was half Norman by blood and much more than half by upbringing, and he must have spent much of the previous 31 years speaking French, so the kingdom he was to rule must inevitably have seemed a foreign land to him. It could be a mistake however to picture him pining for Normandy. Nineteenth-century writers claimed he had brought large numbers of Normans with him to England, apparently supported by a passage in the *Vita*,[11] but later historians are convinced this was untrue. When he returned in 1041 Edward had apparently brought with him only a close household, which could have been as few as four, just one of whom was a Norman, though doubtless they were all French speakers. Probably closest to the king was Robert Champart, abbot of Jumieges, the only Norman in the party, who was to feature largely in the crisis during which England's first castle was recorded in the *Chronicle*. There were also two other clerics; Leofric, an Englishman educated abroad, and Herman.

The other member of the household was Ralph of Mantes, Edward's nephew, son of his sister Godgifu and Drogo, count of Valois and part of the Vexin, a disputed region on the border of Normandy, whose capital was at Mantes in northern France. It was at Mantes that William I received fatal injuries in 1087, when the by then corpulent conqueror fell off his horse while besieging the town, but relations with the duke were good in Ralph's day. His father died in 1035 while accompanying Duke Robert I on a pilgrimage to the Holy Land, and Ralph was himself partly Norman, from his grandmother Emma. He had an impeccably illustrious ancestry, being a descendant of Charlemagne in his father's line and Alfred the Great in his mother's, but he was undoubtedly a younger son, not expected to inherit his father's lands and no doubt hoping for an estate in England. Ralph's date of birth is disputed, but has been put at about 1027,[12] which would have made him about 14 years old in 1041, when he probably came to England with Edward. What their relationship was is unknown, but the fact that Ralph was one of only two of his European relatives that Edward chose to bring with him speaks volumes for his affection for his nephew.

Others may also have come with him, or joined him soon afterwards, including two who became important landowners: Robert fitz Wymarc, a Breton and apparently a kinsman of Edward, who owned land in Essex, and Ralf the 'staller', an officer in the king's household, who was probably also a Breton, and was appointed earl of East Anglia by William the Conqueror. Edward's biographer suggested[13] that he may in fact have had something of a grievance against the Norman court. True, the duchy had offered him hospitality as a boy, but it was fairly parsimonious hospitality: no land, no title, no revenues with which to support himself. In contrast, Henry of Huntingdon said Baldwin provided his mother with an estate at Bruges when she was exiled in Flanders. Edward may well have felt that he could have been better treated in Normandy, but that did not change his Norman blood or his Norman upbringing. By culture and habit of mind he was no Anglo-Saxon, and worse still, according to his biographer,[14] it appeared he mistrusted Scandinavians, which was unfortunate considering the Anglo-Danish make-up of his court.

Of Edward's immediate relations with his chief advisers, the most powerful men in England, we know nothing, though it is possible that delays in receiving their support around the country could explain the delay in his coronation. What is certain is that the three leading earls – Godwine, Leofric of Mercia and Siward of Northumbria – were Cnut's men by appointment and habit of loyalty, and the most important of them was Godwine, to whom Edward owed his crown. Godwine had assiduously amassed lands during the three Anglo-Danish reigns – by 1051, and probably by Edward's accession, he held Kent, Sussex and Wessex, and he was to achieve a massive expansion of this wealth in Edward's reign, such that Domesday Book showed his family were richer than the king.[15] This was in part because Cnut had gifted Wessex, the traditional support and power base of West Saxon kings, to his favourite Godwine, leaving Edward without the revenues and personal support that all his predecessors down to Aethelred had enjoyed. He still had some income from the royal demesnes, but he lacked the personal service of loyal thegns his forerunners had taken for granted. 'His power as king' wrote Professor Barlow, 'was to depend on the extent to which he could utilize the authority of earls who mostly had no tradition of loyalty either to him or to his family'.[16]

Godwine's marriage to Gytha served to emphasise the extent to which the country had become Anglo-Danish. She was Cnut's sister-in-law, the sister of Ulf who had married Cnut's sister Estrith, and daughter of the legendary warrior Thurgils Sprakaleg. Before Edward's accession she had produced six sons and three daughters whose names were a mixture of Danish and Anglo-Saxon. The three eldest boys, Swein, Harold and Tostig, probably born in the second half of the 1020s, all had Scandinavian names, as did two of the girls, Gytha and Gunhild, who were probably born about 1030 and 1035, though Gytha's name would be Anglicized to Edith (Eadldgyth), and she is always referred to in that way by historians. The three younger boys had Anglo-Saxon names, Gyrth, Leofwine and Wulfnoth, probably after Godwine's father, as did the younger girl, Aelfgifu; all were probably born by about 1040.[17] This gave Godwine a large brood of potential young earls, and he lost no time in consolidating the power of his family under Edward, obtaining substantial interest on the loan of goodwill which had swept Edward onto the throne.

By the time of Edward's coronation Godwine's eldest son, Swein, was probably in his early 20s and was said to have received a substantial earldom at the assembly on that occasion, comprising Oxfordshire, Gloucestershire, Herefordshire, Somerset and Berkshire. In 1045 it was Harold's turn and he received an earldom comprising Essex, East Anglia, Cambridgeshire and Huntingdonshire. By 1051, south of The Wash only a narrow central sliver of the envious Mercian kingdom, which formerly controlled most of Swein's lands and in Alfred's day dominated the west as far north as the mouth of the Ribble, broke the iron chain of Godwineson rule.

Godwine was also depicted in later accounts as a despoiler of church lands, though this was always an easy charge for a wealthy man's enemies to make. Two humorous stories of this kind were included in the satirical collection, *The Trifles of Courtiers*, by twelfth-century archdeacon of Oxford, Walter Map. In one, Godwine obtained the nunnery of Berkeley by sending an attractive nephew who so debauched the nuns that the nunnery was closed and the king gave the land to Godwine. The other story is told admirably by Professor Barlow: 'He [Godwine] said to the archbishop of Canterbury, whose manor it was, "Lord do you give me Bosham?" And when the startled prelate answered questioningly, "I give you Bosham?", the earl and his men fell at his feet, kissed them and gave him profuse thanks for his gift.'[18] Whether there is any truth in these stories is anyone's guess, but Domesday Book showed that Godwine had held Berkeley in Gloucestershire and Bosham in Sussex. Nor did the family eschew other forms of revenue. William of Malmesbury had a somewhat confused story in which Godwine's wife, Gytha, was accused of slave-trading, exporting beautiful young English slave girls to Denmark where they would fetch a high price. Whatever the truth of that story, it was very likely that the family were involved in trading slaves to Viking-controlled Ireland, and perhaps even had an Irish 'export manager' in their household, since eldest daughter Edith was said to speak fluent Irish.[19]

In the first act of Edward's reign recorded by the *Chronicle*, he was directly supported by Godwine, Leofric and Siward. The Worcester version of the *Chronicle* said that the three most powerful magnates in the land personally accompanied him to Winchester in mid-November 1043, and stripped his mother of much of her wealth, leaving her only enough to support herself. They took 'all the lands which his mother owned, and … all she owned in gold and in silver and in untold things, because earlier she had kept it from him [Edward] too firmly'. William of Malmesbury later wrote, on good authority as he suggested, that Emma 'had for a long time mocked at the needy state of her son … besides, accumulating money by every method, she had hoarded it, regardless of the poor, to whom she would give nothing, for fear of diminishing her heap'.

John of Worcester said Edward had taken this step on the advice of the earls, but why should the three most powerful noblemen in the land be interested in what essentially seemed to be a family matter? For the earls this act was probably precipitated by fears that Emma had agreed to finance an invasion of England by Magnus of Norway. She may well have been in correspondence with Magnus, and certainly had the wealth to support him, had she chosen to do so. Historians generally now regard her as innocent of the charge, and point out that Magnus had his hands full trying to resist the claims to Denmark of Swein Estrithson, the son of Cnut's sister Estrith and the Danish earl Ulf, but Magnus undoubtedly claimed, whether justly or not, that his treaty with Harthacnut gave him rights to the throne of England, and he continued to be regarded by contemporaries as a serious threat to England right up to his death in 1047. Leaving a possible wealthy supporter of Magnus with funds sufficient to finance an invasion of England was probably a risk that the earls were unwilling to take. Godwine had an additional reason to deny Magnus any possible support, since Swein Estrithson was his nephew.

For Edward this act may have been motivated by his need for funds for the royal treasury, but it may also have been revenge for his mother's part in luring Alfred to his death, which he probably never forgave, and it may well have been revenge for the years that he and his brother wandered as poor relations while his mother amassed wealth in England. Did Edward bide his time over the years, waiting for a chance to take revenge on her, and if so, was he also biding his time to take revenge on Godwine for Alfred's death? This is one intriguing possibility in the events leading up to the crisis of 1051 and the building of England's first castle, and if the murder of his brother wasn't a strong enough motive for Edward's revenge on Godwine, he soon had another.

By 1045, wrote historian Osbert of Clare, '… when the whole government of the kingdom slept in peace, there was a discussion about the consort who should cleave to the royal side'.[20] There followed a description of a fairy tale search for a perfect partner, reminiscent of the *Encomium*'s description of Cnut's search for a wife:

> ... it was decided to seek a wife worthy of so great a husband from among the daughters of the magnates. One alone was found in that people, inferior to none, superior to all, who was recommended both by the distinction of her family and the ineffable beauty of her surpassing youth.

As with Cnut and Emma, there was only ever one candidate, who in this case was of course 'the eldest of the daughters of the illustrious Earl Godwine'. Henry of Huntingdon had Godwine plotting to marry Edith to the ill-fated Alfred as long ago as 1036, when she was probably only about six years old, which made the charge somewhat unlikely, but by 1045 she would have been at least 15 years old and possibly older, and therefore very much of marriageable age in those times. This was undoubtedly the ultimate prize for Godwine. He had risen from obscure beginnings to the highest pinnacle of power and wealth in England, but Edith's marriage to Edward would make him the grandfather of a king of England and ancestor to a line of kings – at least that was doubtless the plan.

The marriage took place on 23 January 1045, thus surely fulfilling Godwine's dearest wish. Edward's bride was apparently the finest flowering of all the feminine virtues, though it has to be borne in mind that views of her are all likely to be based on the description in the *Vita*, the work that she commissioned. This is a sample of the description on offer:

> ... this exquisite young woman was from infancy immersed in the study of letters in the monastery at Wilton, and, it was reported, shone not only in letters, but in her handicraft and the integrity of all her behaviour. Christ had indeed prepared her for His beloved Edward, kindling in her from very childhood the love of chastity, the hatred of vice, and the desire for virtue ... Fair she was in face and even fairer in her faith, quite outstanding in both body and soul, most intelligent and a skilful and ready counsellor.

There was much more of this. What emerged was a portrait of an attractive young woman who achieved perfection in all things, which must have been the view of herself that she wished to be published, since she had commissioned the writer. She could also be seen through modern eyes however as perhaps rather too serious for her young years, perhaps a bit of a prig.

Her new husband was by then close to 40, an advanced age at that time as his description in the *Vita* makes clear: '... of outstanding height, and distinguished by his milky, white hair and beard, full face and rosy cheeks, thin white hands, and long translucent fingers'. It is significant that the marriage was taking place some 30 months after Edward was acclaimed as king and more than 20 months after he was crowned. Historians who wish to argue that Edward owed no particular debt to Godwine suggest that this was not an unusual delay between accession and marriage: Edith's biographer, Pauline Stafford, for example, quoted a number of instances where monarchs were unmarried for extended periods.[21] We can surely agree though, that a 30-month delay did not suggest a man in a hurry to marry. It might in fact suggest a man who was reluctant to marry, and if so then Edward may have had good reason, though that is also a controversial aspect of the relationship. The basis for controversy here revolves around the two essential questions of Edward's marriage to Edith: had Edward taken a vow of chastity as a young man, and if so, did he continue to observe it in his marriage? Was Edward in fact forced into an unwelcome and abhorrent marriage in order to repay his debt to Godwine?

The evidence, such as it is, is unclear and regarded as unreliable, not least because it comes from the anonymous *Vita*, though this is inevitable because, as its translator points out, the *Vita* 'is the only authority for much of our knowledge of Edward the Confessor's appearance, character, habits and religious life'.[22] The evidence for Edward's chastity is inevitably coloured by two factors: Edward and Edith's marriage was childless, and a cult quickly began to surround Edward after his death which caused him to be canonized and become England's patron saint for several centuries. Though Edward was believed to have taken a vow of chastity as a young man in Normandy there is no evidence from that source, but such a vow would have been regarded as laudable in an age of monasticism, and rumours of an unconsummated marriage could have been circulating as early as 1051. Though chastity was never imputed to Cnut, the 'heathen' Dane, his reverence for monasticism was emphasised in the *Encomium*. It would have been natural at that time to think of a young man from a Christian royal dynasty who received his early education in a monastery as embracing the spirit of monastic rule, including celibacy.

According to the *Vita*, Edward's celibacy may have been foretold before his accession. Brihtwald, the aged bishop of Wiltshire, was said to have had a vision about the succession in which he saw St Peter 'consecrate the image of a seemly man as king, assign him the life of a bachelor'.[23] This could mean that Brihtwald envisaged the succession of Edward and knew of some reason why he might choose not to marry, such as a vow of chastity taken in his youth, though bachelor could, of course, have several meanings, including unmarried, but also perhaps living the life of a single man though married. The *Vita* emphasised the father–daughter nature of

Edward's relationship with Edith and noted, 'he preserved with holy chastity the dignity of his consecration, and lived his whole life dedicated to God in true innocence',[24] though what exactly that means in relation to Edward's marriage is very much open to question. Professor Barlow regarded it as an 'inapposite and unproductive' application of theological thinking new at that time. In his introduction to the *Vita*, the professor insisted that 'the evidence for Edward's lifelong celibacy is not very strong'.[25] He pointed out that many contemporaries ignored it and William of Malmesbury seemed 'to have looked at it askance', which indeed he did, though perhaps not quite for the reasons the professor seemed to be suggesting. 'When dying, in the time of King William,' said the twelfth-century historian, 'she [Edith] voluntarily satisfied the bystanders as to her unimpaired chastity by an oath'. This is often seen as an affirmation by Edith of Edward's chastity, since William added, 'the king so artfully managed, that he neither removed her from his bed, nor knew her after the manner of men', but it was not Edward's celibacy that William was looking askance at, but Edith's, since, 'both in her husband's lifetime, and afterwards, she was not entirely free from suspicion of dishonour.' It has to be said that the evidence for Edith's dishonour was not very strong, but it might well be suspected of an attractive young woman in a cold marriage with an older man.

If Edith was circulating rumours in the 1060s of a chaste marriage, as her modern biographer suggested she was,[26] then this may have been intended to prove her own chastity as much as Edward's, especially since their marriage was childless, but this hardly disproves his chastity. This may be an instance where the experts are being 'too expert', too suspicious of their sources. The fact that it could be advantageous for Edward's wife to wish to say that he had taken a vow of chastity, and that she had remained a virgin throughout their marriage, does not automatically suggest that she must therefore be lying.

Plainly we don't know, and can never know, the facts of this case, yet there is evidence to suggest the truth of Edith's claims, and slim as it may be, it is compelling. Firstly, there is not a single instance in any chronicle or history of Edward being noted as wenching or having a mistress. It could be argued that such material was most often written after a monarch's death, and in Edward's case it may have been suppressed because of growing evidence of his sanctity, but there were no such qualms about Olaf Haroldson, who became St Olave, or about Cnut, whose piety was much mentioned, and both of them had at least one mistress; in fact they had the same mistress at various times. There were several accusations made against Edward after his death, which were regarded as particularly damning by contemporaries. They were subsequently dealt with by William of Malmesbury: 'The monasteries were deprived of their monks; unjust sentences were passed by depraved men; his mother's property, at his command, was almost entirely taken from her', but these injustices, said William, were 'extenuated by his followers', by blaming the former charges on Godwine and his sons, and the fate of his mother's property on her parsimony. The former, especially 'the ruin of the monasteries', was arguably a more important charge for a churchman than simply having a mistress, which could easily have been excused by his frustration at his barren marriage or the marital failure of his wife. So it appears there were no mistresses, which may not in itself strengthen the case for Edward having taken a vow of chastity, but it certainly doesn't weaken it.

Secondly, the long delay of up to 30 months before the new king married was remarkable, considering that a child was needed to ensure the succession. It does not suggest a man keen to wed, and may well suggest a man who married under pressure, when he eventually ran out of excuses to put it off. Finally, and most compellingly, Edward repudiated his wife as soon as possible. Within at most a year of the marriage she no longer appeared as a witness to charters,[27] which was a definite affront to her position and probably also meant that Edward refused to have her present at royal engagements, and as soon as an opportunity arose, in late 1051, Edward packed her off to a convent. This is powerful evidence that, whatever the cause, Edward's marriage was, or became, hateful to him and he had long awaited and desired an opportunity to divest himself of his wife. His modern biographer accused Edith of being domineering,[28] and said her childlessness may have 'destroyed the little interest that Edward had in her as a woman'. Sir Frank Stenton wrote: '… the real character of their relations is shown by the energy with which he set himself to overthrow the earl at the first moment when an opportunity came his way'.[29] Whatever the cause, Edward's marital dissatisfaction was the end of Godwine's hopes of becoming the grandfather to a king, and another motive for Edward's revenge upon him.

The character of the king, and thus his relations with his in-laws, was also controversial. Stenton wrote: 'The king's personality is an enigma, and different historians have come to very diverse opinions about his character and ability.'[30] To Stenton he was probably underestimated, with 'reserves of latent energy' beneath his benign manner. William of Malmesbury's claim that Edward, 'from the simplicity of his manners' was 'little calculated to govern', seems to have been based on later views of his piety, but Edward's white hair, and the mild manners he must have been forced to cultivate during his years as a poor relation at European courts, may have given the impression of a man whose personality was less than forceful. William, like Edward of mixed Saxon and Norman parentage, noted that even in the following century opinion of the king's relations with his new in-laws was still split on racial lines; Saxons saying that Godwine and his sons 'were men of liberal mind, the steadfast promoters and defenders of the government of Edward', while Normans insisted they 'acted with the greatest want of respect to the king, aiming at equal sovereignty with him, often ridiculing his simplicity, often hurling the shafts of their wit against him.'

Harold seems to have been the son most often at court with Godwine, and while descriptions of the father make him more a duplicitous statesman than a man of action, Harold seems to have been much more representative of his Danish warrior heritage. The *Vita* described him as tall, handsome and graceful; very much in the mould of Edmund Ironside, a natural soldier able to act with intelligence and guile and command men with his easy charm and good humour, though he could be 'rather too generous with oaths' when angered.[31] There is no illustration or description of Godwine's physical appearance, but Harold may well have taken after his father, and no doubt they would have been a formidable contrast to the pious monarch. The *Chronicle* recorded only one instance in the first six years of Edward's reign in which he defied Godwine: the 1047 request by Godwine's nephew Swein Estrithson in Denmark for naval assistance against Magnus of Norway, which could safely be refused because Leofric and all the court were against it. If the Normans were right, then it could be thought that the mild-mannered Edward's regular humiliation by the sarcastic Godwinson hard men must have kept alive his dreams of revenge on his tormentors.

Given that he would have received a knight's training in Normandy in his youth, there may have been another, more physical, powerful, decisive, 'macho' man inside Edward, trying to get out – perhaps a man more like his heroic half-brother, Edmund Ironside, who had fought Cnut in 1016 until the Dane felt forced to agree upon a settlement. In the years following his accession however, with Godwine's power in the ascendant, that man was having some difficulty getting out. Edward could profitably have promoted Leofric's power as a counterbalance to Godwine's, to divide his powerful earls and ensure that he could rule effectively, but he clearly felt powerless to prevent Godwine's family swallowing up what had formerly been Mercian lands, to make themselves so powerful that the Worcester version of the *Chronicle*, looking back on this period, said that Godwine had 'ruled the king and all England'. Given the humiliations doubtless heaped on him during his wandering years, it is possible that Edward spent much of his reign not certain who he was or should be, torn between the pious supplicant he had become and the man of action he had probably dreamed of being. The fits of anger, referred to by the *Vita*,[32] provide further evidence of a man frustrated at his inability to assert himself as he would have wished. There is, as we will see later, some evidence to suggest that Edward harboured an illusory view of himself as a warrior prince; 'illusory' because he did not take the opportunities doubtless open to him in his youth to go out and make his fortune by the sword in foreign lands. In fact he never at any time showed a taste for the 'death or glory' warrior life. As his biographer Professor Barlow pointed out, 'Edward is not usually regarded as a warrior king; but he may well have been a thwarted hero'.[33]

Thus Edward must have seemed to Godwine to pose little threat to his ambitions, but threats would come, and from closer to home. For Godwine, as for his master Cnut, the destruction of all he had built would largely be wrought by his own family.

Chapter Five

The Final Act

The chain of events leading to Godwine's downfall began as early as 1046, when his eldest son, Swein, took an army into Wales. Since its colonization by Celts after Anglo-Saxon settlement in England, Wales had experienced an evolutionary political process somewhat akin to that across the border, with warring petty kingdoms vying for control of territory, though the geography of Wales lent itself less to attempts at nation building. Late twelfth-century writer Gerald of Wales described the major political divisions of his country in this way:

> From time immemorial Wales has been divided into three more or less equal parts. When I say equal I mean in value rather than in size. These are Gwynedd, or North Wales; South Wales, called in Welsh Deheubarth, which really means Right-Hand Wales, a sub-section of which, containing seven cantrefs, has been given the name of Demetia or Dyfed; and Powys, which is the middle and stretches eastwards.[1]

Anglo-Saxon lords in the west had often nibbled at the boundaries of Wales, and Cnut and a number of his West Saxon predecessors had claimed hegemony over the principality, but it was not until Edward I's campaign in the 1280s that it was fully conquered. In 1046 it was split between two rival rulers, Gruffydd ap Llewelyn, king of Gwynedd and Powys, and the king of South Wales, Gruffydd ap Rhydderch. Border raiding in both directions was a fact of life for Welsh and English, and two of Swein's counties, Herefordshire and Gloucestershire, bordered South Wales, from whence border raiders most often came. With tension apparently rising between these two warlike princes Swein may have feared that hostilities could spill over into his earldom, but it was hardly the time for meddling in Welsh politics. That was exactly what Swein did however. Joining forces with the northern king, he marched into South Wales and demanded hostages from Gruffydd ap Rhydderch as a surety of his future good conduct. This aggressive posturing would cost Herefordshire dear in the future, but Swein would not be there to see it, and it was what he did next that would cost him, and ultimately his father, everything they had.

Fresh from his triumph in Wales, Swein returned through the small north Herefordshire market town of Leominster. He might well have been cheered through the streets by the local populace, believing his actions would make Welsh raids on their town much less likely. This would be heady stuff for a young man in his early twenties, and it may have encouraged him in an action which would bring down the wrath of the establishment upon him. He had apparently admired Eadgifu, the abbess of the convent at Leominster, who may have been a kinswoman of Cnut's nephew, Hakon, who was formerly earl of Worcester.[2] This would have made her a very suitable bride – had she not been a nun. Swein may have gone that way from Wales in order to see her, and in a fit of hubris he had her carried off, seducing her and making her his mistress. Winning a bride by forcefully carrying her off was common enough at that time, especially in the Scandinavian world of which Swein's half-Danish parentage made him a part, but carrying off an abbess from her convent went far beyond what was acceptable. She may even have borne him a son, though the historian who suggested this possibility thought it unlikely.[3] For contemporaries there would have been no mitigation for such a scandalous act, but to us it may be important that Swein appeared to have had real feelings for the lady. The Abingdon chronicler said contemptuously that he 'kept her as long as it suited him, and afterwards let her travel home', but John of Worcester, presumably relying on sources since lost, said Swein had wanted to marry Eadgifu but was not permitted to do so, which seems closer to the truth. In a diocesan record,[4] eleventh-century Worcester monk Heming noted that Swein kept Eadgifu with him for a year, only sending her back to her convent when he was forced to release her by pressure from Bishop Lyfing of Worcester, in whose diocese Leominster lay, backed by Archbishop Eadsige, who had crowned Edward.

There is no record of Godwine's reaction to this incident, but he can hardly have been happy about it. Even though he was no churchman it must have been a severe embarrassment to him at court, and the weakening of his position, which must have resulted, gave Edward the first opportunity to begin to turn the tables on his powerful subject. In the circumstances, there must have been family pressure on Swein to go abroad, probably in 1047, until it had all blown over. Historians generally assume that Swein was outlawed, though there is no mention of this in the *Chronicle*, which usually recorded such things, and had recorded the cause of Swein's downfall. Perhaps Godwine had managed to persuade the king that voluntary exile would be sufficient punishment, though it does seem likely that some judgement was passed on Swein in his absence. Swein went first to Bruges and spent the winter under the protection of the hospitable Baldwin of Flanders, a long-standing ally of Godwine, but in the summer of 1048 he went to his mother's homeland, where his cousin Swein Estrithson had been fighting for his life as king of Denmark against Magnus of Norway. Unfortunately he couldn't keep out of trouble there either, and in the following year the Worcester chronicler noted that Swein had 'ruined himself with the Danes'. At some stage during his absence Swein was deprived of his lands in England, possibly at the behest of other members of his family, suggesting that the fallout from his scandalous seduction of Eadgifu had made him distinctly unpopular at home. Perhaps his subsequent unpopularity with the Danes was the result of trying to gain some advantage by involving himself in the national rivalry on behalf of Norway.

No longer welcome in Denmark, Swein Godwineson headed for England in the summer of 1049, hoping to persuade the king to reinstate him. Details differed in accounts of what followed, but the incident was widely recorded and all accounts agreed on the main events. The king was at Sandwich with a large naval force, in support of the emperor, after Baldwin of Flanders had joined a rebellion against him. Other nations had also heeded the emperor's call and sent forces to Europe, including the Danes, finally united under Swein Estrithson after Magnus's death in 1047. England's role was only to cut off any possible escape by Baldwin. Swein sailed into Bosham with seven or eight ships, whose crews had presumably been persuaded to serve him on promise of payment when he was restored. He made his way to Sandwich and promised the king that he would serve him faithfully, though both the Worcester and Abingdon chroniclers suggested he was lying. Some sources said that the king flatly refused all his requests; the 'Godwineist' Canterbury chronicler alone said that he 'made peace with the king, and he was promised that he should be restored to every honour that he had previously held'; but all agreed that his family prevented it. Instead of an earldom, Swein was given four days to return to his ships and leave England. There are no records of what had happened to Swein's lands during his absence but some if not all had apparently been shared out amongst his family, including Harold and their cousin Beorn, brother of Swein Estrithson of Denmark and nephew of Cnut and Godwine, who had received an unknown earldom at some point during this period, probably thanks to Godwine taking the opportunity to extend family landholdings. Harold undoubtedly opposed Swein's reinstatement, and Beorn also, according to most accounts, though he was apparently more soft-hearted than Harold, or just didn't know the devious Swein as well as his brother, and wanted to help the exile.

Swein's next act must have shocked even his family, mirroring as it did the murder of Alfred in 1036, when Swein was about 10 years old. On some pretext he persuaded Beorn to go with him to his ships, but he then had his cousin seized and carried aboard bound. They sailed along the coast to Dartmouth, where Beorn was murdered and his body was thrown into a deep ditch. It was left to Harold to recover the body of his trusting cousin, and see it buried with dignity in Winchester, near Beorn's uncle, Cnut. Swein's motive for this murder was presumably revenge for Beorn's support of Harold against him, but it was a mean-spirited and spiteful act which was bound to bring swift retribution. Edward could have outlawed Swein, but the miscreant now had no choice but to leave the country, and if he was already exiled then a further similar sentence would be meaningless. Edward assembled the English forces at Sandwich and Swein was declared nithing, a Scandinavian judgement showing he was regarded as a scoundrel, a man without honour, because of his treacherous act. This was a remarkable judgement for an English assembly to pass, perhaps showing how pervasive Danish influence had become after Cnut, since it had no force in English law, and was purely a moral judgement of the kind a Viking assembly might pass on one of their number who was no longer welcome in their midst. But all present would have been aware that it was a sentence which would make Swein an outcast throughout the northern world. Two of his crews had already been slaughtered by the men of Hastings. Deserted by all but two of the remaining crews, Swein returned to Bruges and the protection of the long-suffering Baldwin. Interestingly, none of this is reported in the *Vita*, commissioned by Edith to chronicle her family, offering further proof, if it were needed, of Swein's utter rejection by his brothers and sisters; in fact he is not mentioned anywhere in the book.

It was in July or August of that same year that the king of South Wales, Gruffydd ap Rhydderch, probably taking advantage of the absence of the local militia on duty in the south, took revenge for Swein's action against him in 1046, by joining forces with a substantial Viking raiding party from Ireland which had sailed up the Usk in 36 ships. Together they crossed the Wye and burnt a border settlement, killing all the inhabitants they could find. This action clearly took the English by surprise, while their attention had been concentrated elsewhere. The new bishop of Worcester, Ealdred, hastily gathered what men were available from Gloucestershire and Herefordshire and, said John of Worcester, the English supplemented their forces with Welshmen, presumably from the border area, who swore loyalty but were actually in league with Gruffydd. The raiders launched a dawn attack and slaughtered many of the defenders; the bishop and other survivors fled in confusion. There was nothing now to prevent the attackers raiding at will throughout Herefordshire, but they seem to have contented themselves with the victory and the booty they had doubtless already seized, since there is no mention in the chronicles of further attacks. Fear of a similar opportunistic attack two years later may have been a major factor in the events leading to the building of England's first castle.

Godwine's standing must by now have been badly damaged by Swein's actions, though not as badly as it would be, but he still must have been torn over the fate of his eldest son. It is quite possible that his brother Harold and sister Edith were happy to leave Swein where he was and forget about him, but for Godwine, allowing his first born to languish in perpetual exile may have been more than he could bear. When, later in the year, the king sent Ealdred, the bishop of Worcester, to Rome, it was an opportunity to try again for a reconciliation. Ealdred will have known Swein, since his see covered part of Swein's earldom, and he could easily pass through Flanders on his way home again in 1050. We don't know what passed between them, but Swein must have been contrite about his debauching of an abbess, and Ealdred brought him back to England and secured a reconciliation with the king, under which Swein recovered his title and some of his lands, apparently including Herefordshire. Edward's biographer, Frank Barlow, called the pardoning of Swein 'extraordinary', as well he might since this was a complete reversal of Edward's position of the previous year and the irreparable moral judgement which had been passed on Swein for the murder of his kinsman Beorn. Professor Barlow added: 'Edward may still have thought that by pardoning Swein he was really injuring the family'.[5]

Clearly Godwine now owed a substantial debt to the king for the reinstatement of his reprobate son, and Edward was already seeing himself finally winning the battle of wills with Godwine and his family. His new-found strength was seen mainly in his award of ecclesiastical appointments. The church had a key role in Anglo-Saxon society. Bishops rivalled earls in their civil power, making it perhaps inevitable that magnates such as Godwine should be involved in tussles over church landholdings, which were not always honestly acquired on either side. In many respects bishops led civil society, and could as readily be found sitting in civil councils and even leading men in battle, as Ealdred had done against the Welsh in 1049, as officiating in their sees. Thus ecclesiastical appointments were a prime means of establishing a power base, either for a king or a powerful subject. The appointees to vacant sees and abbots' chairs would usually come from within the monasteries at that time, since there were generally no candidates outside the monastic sphere with the learning and ecclesiastical grounding to successfully fill the roles.

Edward had begun to place his own people in these roles. On the death in 1049 of Eadnoth, the bishop of Oxfordshire, Edward had given the see to his priest Ulf, which the Abingdon chronicler called 'a bad appointment'. The Worcester chronicler added that he was subsequently expelled from the see 'because he did nothing like a bishop in it, so much so that we

are ashamed to say anything more about it'. It was in the following year
however that Edward made the appointment which would lead almost
directly to the crisis of 1051. The monk Robert of Jumieges, who had come
to England with Edward, was already regarded as the king's chief adviser, and
would thus have been looked on with some suspicion by magnates such as
Godwine, who will have resented his influence with the king. Now Edward
placed the Norman monk in the vacant see of London and, said the *Vita*,
'with the authority derived from this promotion [he] intruded himself more
than was necessary in directing the course of the royal councils and acts',
causing much resentment as a result.[6] William of Malmesbury later wisely
wrote, 'the English are scornful of any superior and the Normans cannot
endure an equal'. An element of xenophobia may therefore have soured
relations, but the antipathy of Godwine and his sons to anyone threatening
their power probably applied as much to Saxons as to Normans.

On 29 October 1050 the venerable Eadsige, the archbishop of Canterbury
who had crowned Edward, died. The power of this position was hard to
underestimate, the holder being second only to the king in England, and
sometimes not even that, since he drew European power from the pope.
This major appointment was of course firmly based on Godwine's territory
and he had just the man for the job. A monk at Canterbury named Aethelric
was said to be the choice of the monastery there and fortuitously was a
kinsman of Godwine.[7] There was a time when the king would doubtless
have acquiesced to Godwine's choice, but that time was past. Instead the
king appointed the hated Norman, Robert of Jumieges, as archbishop of
Canterbury. Robert then had to journey to Rome to have his appointment
confirmed by the pope, but by 29 June 1051 he was back, possibly
accompanied by other Normans whom he had encouraged to return with
him, and ready to deal with Godwine. Their rivalry for the ear of the king
in past years had clearly engendered a great deal of ill will between these
two men,[8] and Robert may have been encouraged by Edward in his enmity
to the earl. Said the *Vita*: 'The archbishop ... began to provoke and oppose
the earl with all his strength and might ... He often attacked Godwine with
schemes, and when he found him deserted by fortune vexed him with not
a few injuries'.[9]

One cause of friction was land belonging to the monastery at Canterbury
which Godwine had taken for himself, and even the Godwineist *Vita*
admitted that the archbishop was in the right in that argument. Robert
then went further, resurrecting the old charge of Alfred's murder against
Godwine, and trying to convince the king that the earl was plotting a
similar fate for him.[10] As the summer wore on it must have seemed that
Godwine's meteoric rise was about to be followed by an equally swift and
disastrous fall. If the charge of murder could be made to stick this time, then

Godwine could be deprived of all his landholdings, and the power of his family would be destroyed, which is what Robert and the king no doubt intended. Edward must have felt the yoke of Godwineist power slipping off his shoulders, and he may already have been planning the new design which appeared on coins in the following year, replacing his former debased classical image with that of a virile, bearded warrior in a battle helmet.[11] It was Edward's victory fanfare. But Godwine had not achieved his high position without learning how to combat adversity.

It must have been in late July or early August that Godwine pulled off the masterstroke which completely turned the tables on Edward and his Norman archbishop. He announced the forthcoming marriage of his third son, Tostig, to Judith, half-sister of the one man Edward had cause to fear – Baldwin of Flanders. Baldwin was the leader of an important European maritime power, and enmity between the two men had apparently been long-standing. It had been exacerbated by a recent attempt by Edward's kinsman, William of Normandy, leader of the other main European maritime power, to ally the duchy with Flanders through marriage with Baldwin's daughter, though the emperor, still angry with Baldwin over the rebellion, ensured that the pope vetoed the match. Baldwin's hospitable reception of a number of English exiles, including Swein Godwineson, and even a couple of Viking pirates who had made a hit-and-run raid on the south coast in 1048, and were allowed to sell their plunder and slaves in Flanders,[12] had also badly strained relations between the two courts. But more importantly, Baldwin's half-sister and Tostig's bride was Edward's niece, though once removed, which gave their children a tenuous but real claim to the English throne, and the marriage produced an alliance between Godwine's family and the only European maritime power both able and perhaps willing to send a substantial naval force to England in support of the Godwinesons. This was a real danger since Edward, though he could claim service from the seamen of the channel ports, had dismissed all the professional sailors in English service earlier that year.

As ever, there was an element of chance in the creation of this alliance at that time, since Baldwin was then urgently seeking marital alliances to strengthen his hand against the emperor, but Godwine must surely have been quick to see the potential of such an alliance for his family, and it was doubtless a tribute to his persuasiveness that Baldwin accepted the match even though Tostig was not an earl at that time. The count will clearly have understood that he was allying himself not just with Tostig, but with the most powerful family in England. Edward will have realised that the alliance could destroy at a stroke everything he believed he had achieved, and make him more surely a dupe of Godwine's family than he had ever been. Should he resist any demand in the future, he could be threatened with the massive forces the Godwinesons could muster, combined with the land and sea forces of Flanders, which could raise the very real possibility that he might be deposed. It must now have seemed to Edward that all he had won through years of adversity was being suddenly snatched away from him, but perhaps he was now finally able to display the warrior qualities of bold decisiveness which he is likely to have admired in his boyhood heroes. It may have seemed that Godwine had landed the knockout blow, but the bout was not over yet.

During mid August Edward received a visitor whose actions would once more turn the tide of events. Was this a pure coincidence, or the result of a deliberate act by Edward? His state of mind at that time is relevant here. His biographer, Frank Barlow, paints a picture of a man who saw himself as riding a tide of success since Swein's reinstatement in the previous year: '…for twelve months he could not put a foot wrong…as crisis followed crisis, and Edward came stronger out of each, it must have seemed that nothing could break the run of good luck.'[13] Certainly at this point Edward must have felt that he had nothing to lose by gambling, and probably that his luck would see him through to a successful conclusion.

Edward's visitor was Eustace, count of Boulogne, and he was not a stranger; he was Edward's brother-in-law, husband of his sister Godgifu, the daughter of Aethelred and Emma born between 1005 and 1013, who was also the mother of Ralph of Mantes by her first husband. The visit may have been coincidental, but there could have been two or three weeks between Godwine's announcement of Tostig's marriage and Eustace's arrival. It was tight, but there was enough time to send a messenger across the channel and for Eustace to come to England, and this is significant in trying to determine the motivation of those involved in the events that followed. Two chroniclers, in Worcester and in Canterbury, reported on these events, though with considerable differences of detail. John of Worcester also added a few additional details, presumably based on sources we do not have. What we do know without doubt is that there was a bloody incident between the visitors and the people of Dover.

Eustace came into Dover with 'a few ships', said John of Worcester, suggesting the count had brought a suspiciously large body of retainers for a friendly, family visit. The Worcester chronicle described Eustace and his men running into trouble on their arrival, and all English accounts agreed the trouble was started by the aggressive way that Eustace's men demanded lodgings in the town from unwilling citizens. 'His men went foolishly looking for billets and killed a certain man of the town,' said the Worcester chronicler. The quarrel got completely out of hand after a bystander killed one of Eustace's men in revenge. The conflict widened with Eustace and his men charging the townspeople on horseback, and 'much evil was done on either side with horses and with weapons, until the people assembled, and then Eustace's men fled to the king at Gloucester, who granted them protection', said the chronicler. Eustace's men were presumably professional soldiers, but men in the town may well have seen action with the militia or on warships, and will have had their own weapons. Eustace had escaped as the people organised for a full retaliatory attack, with just a few of his men, said the Canterbury chronicler. The Worcester chronicler said seven of Eustace's men had been killed in the bloody clash, the Canterbury chronicler said 19 dead and many wounded, which may be more accurate. John of Worcester later claimed they had killed many men, women and children in the town, which may be an exaggeration, but it was clearly a very bloody incident, though the account of the Worcester chronicler made it appear a chance encounter.

There was however a different version of how this incident began, and the difference could be significant. The Peterborough chronicle, based on a manuscript from Canterbury, which should thus be the most reliable source on these events, claimed the bloody confrontation at Dover broke out only *after* Eustace met the king and held private discussions with him. If this was correct then Edward would have had the opportunity to discuss with his brother-in-law a plan which might disadvantage Godwine, and the events which followed could have been more deliberate than accidental. If the king ordered Godwine to punish the people of Dover for their attitude to Eustace's men, and if Godwine refused, then his fate would be sealed, since disobeying the king was treason. In this version of events Eustace and his men, after departing from the king, travelled to Canterbury where they took a meal break. They then rode towards the port, but 'when he was some miles or more this side of Dover, he put on his mailcoat, and all his companions, and went to Dover'. This extraordinary account suggests that Eustace and his men readied themselves for battle before riding into Dover, presumably expecting or even intending to do battle with the townspeople.

Was Eustace expecting trouble because he had experienced animosity when he passed through the town on his arrival? If so it would have been politic to avoid confrontation, but the chroniclers agreed that the incident was provoked by the unreasonable behaviour of Eustace's men, which suggests it was their deliberate intention to stir up trouble in Dover, either as simple revenge for earlier churlishness by the locals, or perhaps as part of more sinister machinations. If the latter, the differing chronicle versions could suggest that someone had tried to muddy the waters over whether the incident took place before or after Eustace's private discussions with the king, and there is some evidence, albeit circumstantial, to support this view. The Worcester chronicle, which suggested the incident at Dover was a simple disagreement on Eustace's arrival, had a much fuller version of events in London later in the month than the Canterbury chronicle, perhaps implying that the information used by the Worcester chronicler came from someone at or close to the court, and thus that chronicle could contain an element of official 'rewriting' of events. There is some evidence to support this view. Edward's nephew, Ralph of Mantes, had by 1050 apparently become earl of Worcestershire and part of Warwickshire, the former territory of the Hwicca tribe,[14] and he, or someone in his service, may well have been the source for much of the information about this incident in the Worcester chronicle, though he may not have known of his uncle's full intentions. A similar charge could of course be made against the 'Godwineist' Canterbury chronicler, that his version of events was falsely intended to imply a plot by the king against Godwine, but if the family wished to suggest such a plot, the one place where it would be evident would be in the *Vita*, commissioned by Edith, and there is no hint of such a plot there. It might therefore appear that the discrepancy between the *Chronicle* accounts could genuinely disclose a regal plot to reverse Godwine's fortunes.

This raises important questions: not least, was Edward sufficiently ruthless and manipulative a politician to have engineered a political crisis to disadvantage Godwine? Professor Barlow, who chronicled the career of Godwine and his family and wrote the standard biography of Edward the Confessor, though apparently not proposing such a plot, seems to suggest that Edward might have been willing and able to engineer it: 'Edward ... seems to have liked grim jokes and ironical judgements. Simulation and dissimulation were political skills that were highly prized'.[15] Emma Mason, who wrote the other history of the family, is convinced that Edward did engineer this crisis.[16] If we accept that Edward was plotting, this raises other questions, not least, why should Eustace participate in what, for him, could be a risky enterprise?

Barlow's account suggests that the king could have given Eustace good reason to cooperate; in fact the same good reason he had given to various other foreign rulers. Edith's childlessness was responsible for the ultimate failure of Edward's dynasty after his death, but it was also the reason for the outstanding success of his foreign policy while he lived. His lack of a successor meant that, despite dismissing his professional navy, Edward kept England secure during his reign, since he could disarm any foreign aggressor with a 'nod and wink' over the succession. He was known to have made similar empty promises to Godwine's nephew, Swein Estrithson of Denmark in the 1040s, William of Normandy in 1051-2, and his half-nephew Edward the Exile in 1054-7. '[Edward] could have regarded it as a diplomatic card which could be played repeatedly, now recognising Swein Estrithson as his heir, now William of Normandy. Nor need he have limited his play so narrowly.

Diplomatic promises were cheap', said Professor Barlow.[17] There were no doubt a number of others who received such promises, including probably Eustace. Edward's brother-in-law had several reasons to be interested in the succession. By 1051 he is likely to have had a daughter of marital age by Godgifu and any son she had would be Edward's great-nephew and a possible successor to the English throne. It has been suggested that the couple had no issue but Professor Barlow believed they did.[18] Eustace's step-sons, Walter, count of the Vexin on the border of Normandy, and Ralph of Mantes were also potential claimants. 'All this group may have considered that their claim to the English throne was better than William's or Swein's,' said Barlow, '... they were Edward's, as opposed to his mother's or step-father's, kin; and they may well have wanted at this time to know where they stood.' Ms Mason suggested rather different reasons.[19] She believed that Eustace's motivations were his bad relations with Baldwin of Flanders, his desire to secure Godgifu's extensive landholdings in England, following her death about 1049, and to a lesser extent the fact that the murdered Alfred had been his kinsman. If Edward was plotting against Godwine, then it appeared that Eustace had good reasons to agree to take a part.

As ever, the conspiracy theory of history is unlikely to be entirely true, but it may not be entirely false either. If Eustace had visited the king before the incident at Dover, and mentioned to his brother-in-law his anger with the churlish attitude of the townspeople of Dover, then it is quite possible that Edward may have seen in that situation the seeds of Godwine's downfall. It is unlikely that either man realised how bloody the incident would become, but this would have been to Edward's advantage. The usual punishment for the citizens of Dover would be to 'harry' the town, almost in the manner of a Viking raid: killing all the townspeople that could be found and burning the town. Knowing Godwine as he did, the king must have realised there was little chance he would agree to harry Saxons at an important port in his territory for killing Frenchmen. If Edward did engineer this crisis he was doing so at very little risk. The worst that could have happened was that Godwine might have actually obeyed the order to harry the port, in which case he would have been extremely unpopular in Kent and probably throughout his lands, since Anglo-Saxons might well have looked on this as a fair fight which the citizens of Dover didn't start. This would have further exacerbated the problems Godwine was already labouring under, which would have made him even less of a threat to the king. For Edward, as the Americans say, there seemed to be no downside.

The Worcester chronicler suggested that Godwine began gathering his forces as soon as he heard of the incident in Kent. John of Worcester, following this chronicler, wrote: 'Earl Godwine, taking it hard that such events should happen in his earldom, was moved to very great anger, and mustered an innumerable army from his whole earldom.' The Canterbury chronicler had Godwine summoned to the king at Gloucester, where Edward often held his court. Eustace 'gave him a prejudiced account of how they had fared, and the king grew very angry with the townsmen', and 'sent for Earl Godwine and ordered him to carry war into Kent to Dover.' The *Vita*[20] seemed to suggest that Tostig's nuptials were taking place at this time. Professor Barlow thought this unlikely,[21] but John of Worcester, who may well have had access to sources other than those we now have, clearly says Tostig was married later that month and implies that Judith and Tostig were in England then, though with the sources we have it is not possible to clearly determine this.

Probably neither of the chroniclers had the full facts about Godwine's actions at the start of the crisis. Edward surely must have summoned him to Gloucester at an early stage, but Godwine was sufficiently astute to discern the likely course of events, and it would have been surprising if he had not given orders immediately to call out the militia from his family's lands, which would have been much easier if all the family were present for Tostig's wedding. If he went to the king, which the Canterbury chronicler said he did, then he refused to undertake the expedition into Kent, as Edward could have predicted, 'because it was abhorrent to him to injure the people of his own province'. In fairness to Godwine, the king had taken a very precipitate decision on the matter. This was not a situation of the kind which arose when two of Harthacnut's housecarls were killed in 1041, leading to the harrying of Worcester. Here there was no attack on the crown or its servants, though Edward could have taken the view that an attack on a foreign ruler and his brother-in-law was an affront to him; but it was not clear that the townspeople of Dover would have known who Eustace was, and it was questionable who attacked whom. The facts were by no means clear and the king had heard only one side of the story. If the king's motive was to harm Godwine however, the full facts were irrelevant. It has to be said that there may have been no regal plot; Edward may simply have taken advantage of the events which occurred, but if this was simply a chance chain of events, it was a surprisingly fortuitous one for Edward.

The events which followed however showed that even the best laid plot could quickly go awry. Edward may have had some conception that Godwine would resist, but the violence of his reaction clearly took Edward and the other earls by surprise. Perhaps Godwine also felt he had nothing to lose. Perhaps he had finally been pushed too far and acted in a towering rage. Professor Barlow suggested that was probably his state of mind before the Dover incident: 'The earl was out of favour, was not listened to, and was being harassed by Robert of Jumieges. By the end of the summer he had obviously taken all that he could stand, and it needed only one more affront to provoke a desperate act.'[22] Whatever the reason, Godwine raised the armed men from all his family's lands, which was effectively a royal prerogative, and treated it as his own private army. There was a long Anglo–Saxon tradition of men being called up for service in the militia or fyrd (pronounced feared), but it was essentially for service to the king. The numbers called up were on the basis of the lands held by their lord. The Berkshire Domesday showed it was the custom for one man to be raised for every five hides of land. These men would be the better off amongst the peasant classes, because they were required to serve for 60 days at their own expense and usually expected to provide their own weapons. The fyrd may formerly have been raised by royal command but by Aethelred's reign it could be raised by earls or bishops from their lands. It was still essentially regarded however as a royal war band, but Godwine had now raised the armed men from his lands against the king.

The massive army the Godwinesons raised emphasised how far the family's power had spread in Edward's reign. Godwine's men were drawn from Kent and Sussex and right across Wessex; Swein's men cane from Oxfordshire, Gloucestershire, Herefordshire, Somerset and Berkshire; Harold's men from Essex, East Anglia, Huntingdonshire and Cambridgeshire. It must have taken some days for the whole of this huge force to assemble in Gloucestershire, increasing the likelihood that Godwine had given orders for its mobilisation before he was summoned to the king, and that the family had been gathered together when he received the news from Kent, so that he was able to give his sons immediate orders to begin the call up. The one unanswered question remaining about the king's plot, if there was one, related to Edward's location at the start of the crisis. If he planned a showdown with Godwine, surely he would have wished to face it on safe ground, not in the heart of Godwinson power at Gloucester. Perhaps he wanted to get as far as possible from the 'scene of the crime' in Dover. Perhaps it was a measure of his over-confidence; certainly once he realised the strength of the Godwineson response he moved to London as quickly as possible.

No dates are given by the chroniclers for most of these events. The Canterbury chronicler gave us 29 June 1051 as the date on which Robert of Jumieges, whose 'smear' campaign against Godwine largely caused the political crisis, returned from Rome, confirmed as archbishop of Canterbury. The Worcester chronicler gave us 1 September as the date on which the crisis between king and subject deepened. Within that nine week period, the chroniclers told us, Robert progressed his campaign against Godwine, the earl announced the nuptials of his son Tostig, and Eustace arrived at Dover, met Edward possibly at London, wreaked havoc at Dover and hastened to the king at Gloucester. Given the dates offered by the chroniclers, and the length of time likely to be needed for Robert's campaign against Godwine to take effect, the campaign must have been getting into gear during the course of July, and Godwine is likely to have announced Tostig's marriage in late July or early August.

It is very difficult to determine exact dates for the dramatic events which followed, because in some cases we lack exact locations. We can place Eustace at Dover; he then had a meeting with the king but we don't know where it took place, possibly in London. We know he returned to Dover and subsequently went to Gloucester. We know Godwine was summoned to the king, but we don't know where he was at that time. The one other fact of which we can be certain is that all travel and communication moved at the speed of a horse, which was generally about 25 miles a day.[23] Given time for Eustace to arrive in Dover, whether summoned by Edward or not, for them to meet and for the Dover incident to take place, with travel on horseback between these locations, we can construct a tentative schedule for these events, which should not be too far from the reality. Eustace must have arrived in Dover around 14 August, and assuming that the Dover incident did take place after a meeting with the king in London, it probably happened about 20 August. Godwine probably did not receive the king's summons until late August, but he must have known of the incident by 22-23 August and it is reasonable to assume that he gave orders for his family's forces to be called out around that time, since the chroniclers suggested that the Godwineson forces were in Gloucestershire in early September, and some had to come a considerable distance. John of Worcester said the movement of Godwineson forces 'did not remain secret from King Edward', which was inevitable since he was on Godwineson territory at that time.

It is necessary to combine the annals of the Worcester and Canterbury chroniclers and that of John of Worcester, and fill in the gaps with logical assumptions, to try to get a clear account of events. It was on 1 September 1051 that Godwine met Edward, and it must have been an angry scene, as the king demanded the harrying of Dover and the earl steadfastly refused to co-operate. Edward called a meeting of the whole council for 8 September. John of Worcester suggested a later date for these events, but it has to be assumed that the chroniclers closest to the events would have the most accurate dates. The Godwineson forces, and earls Swein and Harold, began moving into the area very soon after 1 September and encamped at Beverstone, Gloucestershire, on the Bristol to Oxford road, which was possibly the formal meeting place of the Longtree hundred, about 19 miles from the king in Gloucester. On or shortly before 8 September Godwine sent a note to the king and the council, though it is difficult to reconcile the two accounts of what it contained. The Canterbury chronicler said the note suggested that the Godwinesons, and presumably their army, would come to the king and council to seek their advice on how 'they might avenge the insult to the king and the whole nation,' and there is little doubt that they regarded Eustace as the guilty party. The Worcester chronicler claimed they threatened war if the king did not hand Eustace and his surviving men over to them. The note may have embodied both these forms of content of course. There is little doubt that it was intended as a threat; the only question is over how thinly veiled it was. The Worcester chronicler said Godwine also demanded the handing over of 'the Frenchmen who were in the castle,' showing that by that date England's first castle had been built. The details of how, why and where it had been built will be looked at in the following chapters.

Earls Leofric from Mercia and Siward from Northumbria arrived soon afterwards with just personal escorts. Clearly they had no idea of what was happening, which suggested that the massive Godwinson forces were not in place until after the earls were summoned on 1 September. They quickly sent urgent messages to their earldoms for all the militia to be despatched as quickly as possible. Interestingly, there was no mention of the arrival of Ralph of Mantes, Edward's nephew, which suggested that he was already with his uncle in Gloucester – a fact which may be very significant in the story of England's first castle. The arrival of the earls, even minus most of their forces, heartened Edward who, according to John of Worcester, had been 'terrified for a time'. He now sent a message refusing Godwine's demands, and the stage was set for a showdown which could have become a bloodbath, as the northern and Midlands army assembled and the whole of the nation divided into two armed camps, facing each other and ready, even eager, for battle. John of Worcester wrote: '… from all England, all men of standing were on one side or the other'.

It is likely that most Anglo-Saxons saw their loyalty as being to their thegn and their lord. The king must have been a distant figure, and if the men to whom they were loyal ordered them to fight against the king, they would probably have had few qualms about doing so. However, Godwine issued no such order. For a brief period he had the king at his mercy, but he failed to press home his advantage. Perhaps events just moved too fast. Perhaps he hesitated because he was intelligent enough to realise that had he done so, events would have acquired their own momentum. Had he bent the king to his will by threat of military force, he would have been forced to go further and try to turn Edward into a puppet ruler, almost certainly sparking a bitter civil war. So the moment passed and both sides backed away from a conflict which they knew would only weaken the country, to the advantage of its enemies abroad. In the meantime 'foreign men', no doubt including Robert of Jumieges and possibly also other Normans whom he had gathered about him, joined the king and reiterated Robert's charges against Godwine, and the earl now feared treachery if he should try to appear before the council. Instead the two sides agreed to reconvene the council in London on 24 September.

One of the most intriguing aspects of this crisis is the silence of the chroniclers over the charges against Godwine. It is generally assumed that he would be charged before the council with rebellion against the king for refusing to harry Dover, but the accusations of the 'foreign men', mentioned by the Canterbury chronicle, imply other charges. This was confirmed by the *Vita* which did not mention Eustace's visit or the incident at Dover, but said that at Gloucester Edward formally charged Godwine, in his absence, with the murder of his brother Alfred.[24]

For Godwine, his hesitation was to cost him dear. His forces began to melt away, fearing a fight against the king, the archbishop and the most powerful earls in the northern half of England, or perhaps no longer believing the Godwinesons would fight, or could win if they did. Edward had cleverly called out the fyrd from Godwineson lands, which meant the thegns marching for Godwine were forced to join the king. Setting up his base in his manor of Southwark, Godwine must have known he was beaten. He could not now fight and his only chance was to clear his name before the council, but to do so he would have to cross the river and put himself in the power of his political enemies, which he dare not do. Stigand, the bishop of Winchester, was the go-between. Godwine played for time, pleading that hostages be given for his safe conduct, but this was repeatedly refused; Edward had no need to make concessions to a beaten man. Stigand returned with Edward's final answer: that Godwine's demands would be met when the king's brother and all his companions were returned to him alive.

Left with no other option, Godwine and his sons fled from England, leaving Edward triumphant as he outlawed them. Collecting all the valuables they could carry, Godwine and his wife Gytha, Swein, Gyrth, and according to John of Worcester, Tostig and Judith, went to Bosham in Sussex and took ship to Flanders where, like so many other English exiles before them, they became guests of the hospitable Count Baldwin. Harold and Leofwine went to Bristol and took ship for Ireland. Thus Edward drove from Anglo-Saxon England undoubtedly the most powerful family it had ever known, and the Worcester chronicler wrote their epitaph in these words:

> It would have seemed remarkable to everyone who was in England, if anyone earlier told them that it should turn out thus, because he [Godwine] was formerly so very much raised up, as if he ruled the king and all England; and his sons were earls and the king's favourites; and his daughter was married and espoused to the king.

Chapter Six

The Hunt for Osbern's Castle

The crisis of September 1051 revealed the existence – 15 years before the Conquest – of a castle built in England by Normans, but how do we know that it was England's first castle? There are two main forms of evidence that this was the first castle. One will have been arrived at by the end of this chapter. The other is simply that this was the first Norman castle to be recorded by the English chroniclers. There may well be historians who will claim that is insufficient as evidence, and certainly there are gaps in the *Chronicle* record, but we have to trust the chroniclers sufficiently to believe that something as unusual as the first Norman castle in England would have been recorded, and no other was noted prior to September 1051.

This is not conclusive evidence of the kind we would require about present day events, but many accepted tenets of eleventh-century history rest on no greater basis. For example, it is plain from the previous chapter that the character and relationships of Edward, Edith and Godwine, all of which have been regarded as clear and unequivocal by past historians, are open to controversial re-interpretation, yet we know beyond doubt from the *Chronicle*, supported by other contemporary sources, that Edward and Edith did marry, that Edward and Godwine were inevitably forced into a close and less than harmonious relationship, and that a crisis in that relationship did take place in September 1051. Historians may – and doubtless will – argue endlessly about the relative significance of these events, but the essential facts are clear enough. As Sir Frank Stenton, referring to the *Chronicle* material about that first Norman castle, wrote: 'The emphasis laid by the *Chronicle* on the building of a single castle makes it probable, though far from certain, that it was the first work of its kind in the county [Herefordshire]'.[1] And if the first in the county, then the first in the country, since Herefordshire, the West Midlands county bordering Wales, which is famed for its cattle and cider, saw a unique spate of castle building in the months that followed. The sites of these castles, if not the timber with which they were likely to have been built, still survive today, but they are far from being the oldest sites in Britain to which we give the name 'castle'. The question of what constituted a castle, based on its construction and use, is considered in the next chapter, but for the moment it is sufficient to say that the first reports of a Norman castle in September 1051 show that those who saw it realized that they were seeing something quite new to England, something foreign; something that had never before been seen in this land. Fifteen years later, after William's victory at Hastings, Norman castles began to appear across the country, but in 1051 such a thing was unknown in England.

Those first reports of a castle built by Normans were in the Worcester chronicle, the Peterborough chronicle – which originated in Canterbury – and subsequently in John of Worcester's chronicle, but the chroniclers were no more informative about it than they were about the crisis in general, and we have to piece together the details from a handful of annals over the following year to begin to get a picture of what was happening. In September 1051 the Worcester chronicler, perhaps close to the court but far from the action, said simply that Godwine's ultimatum to Edward included a demand for handing over of 'the Frenchmen who were in the castle', with no indication of where it was or when it had been built. The Canterbury annalist gave a more detailed account: 'At this time the foreigners had built a castle in Herefordshire in Earl Swein's territory and inflicted all the injuries and insults they possibly could upon the king's men in that region'. There was no explanation of what these 'injuries and insults' were, and the chroniclers did not name the builder of the castle in Herefordshire, doubtless because they did not then know his name, which suggested that he was not a known figure at court or a landowner of any substance. This situation had clearly changed by the following year, when he was named in *Chronicle* entries. Placing the castle firmly in Swein Godwineson's territory, though not specific, showed that the chronicler wanted to leave no doubt of the offence it was likely to cause to Godwine and his sons; this was clearly regarded as a daring incursion into the territory of the most important and feared family in England.

Godwine's family were not likely to be exiled for long and in 1052 they provoked a further crisis which, said the Canterbury chronicler, caused the Normans, who had no doubt thrived in Godwine's absence, to panic: 'When archbishop Robert and the Frenchmen learnt this, they took their horses, and some went west to Pentecost's [Osbern's] castle, some north to Robert's Castle'. Robert was apparently Robert fitz Wymarc who followed Edward the Confessor to England from Normandy, and may have built his 'castle', probably at Clavering in Essex,[2] in that same period, 1051-2, presumably consolidating a power base in the absence of Godwine and Harold, though it was actually a fortified private residence that he built, rather than a castle,

as we will see in the next chapter. By later that year Osbern, who for the
first time had a by-name or nickname, Pentecost, had apparently acquired
a second castle, commanded by a comrade or more likely by a second
in command, since John of Worcester, in an entry not found elsewhere,
recorded that 'Osbern, nicknamed Pentecost and his comrade Hugo
surrendered their castles'. This sparse chronicle documentation provides all
the direct, contemporary evidence we have for the existence of Osbern
Pentecost's castle. The vagueness of these annals must also beg the question
whether they actually all refer to the same Osbern and the same castle,
but anything else seems unlikely, and historians have accepted that all these
annals do relate to Osbern Pentecost's castle. It was not, however, the only
castle to be built in 1051-2, and since we have no exact location for Osbern's
castle we need to consider whether any of the other castles mentioned were
actually his.

In that same period the Worcester chronicler, or the 'northern chronicler'
as inveterate southerner Sir Frank Stenton insisted on calling him,[3] had
a 1052 annal suggesting the existence of a castle near Leominster, in the
north of Herefordshire. 'Gruffydd the Welsh king raided in Herefordshire,
so that he came very near to Leominster; and men gathered against him,
both local men and the Frenchmen from the castle. And there were killed
very many good men of the English, and also from among the French.' The
castle was presumably in Herefordshire but no precise location was given,
nor any information on the builder. There was also apparently a castle at
Hereford, probably also built in this period, though it was not referred to in
contemporary chronicles. It was mentioned only fleetingly as 'the citadel'
or 'fortress' in translations of the Welsh *Chronicle of the Princes*[4] when a joint
Welsh, Viking and rebel Mercian force sacked the town in 1055, and not at all
in the English sources, though the incident was mentioned in the *Chronicle*.
We have a location here but it is not exact, and again we have no name for
the builder of this castle. Another reference comes from Domesday Book,
compiled 35 years later in 1086. The first post-Conquest earl of Hereford,
that is earl over Herefordshire, William Fitz Osbern, refortified a castle at
Ewyas Harold, now in the extreme south-west of Herefordshire, close to
the Welsh border. Since the castle was refortified soon after the Conquest it
must logically have been in existence before 1066.

There is also mention by John of Worcester of another castle, though a
close look at the facts suggests there is no credible evidence for it, and that
he has simply muddled the reference to Osbern's castle in the chronicles of
1051. John, perhaps misled by the Worcester annalist's lack of detail about 'the
Frenchmen who were in the castle', referred to in Godwine's ultimatum to
Edward during the political crisis of 1051, believed that the castle was 'on the
cliff at Canterbury', manned by 'the Normans and the men of Boulogne'.

John's account has muddied the waters for many professional historians, but there is little doubt that he has got his whole account muddled: his dating for the political crisis is different from that of the two extant contemporary annals, which agree that the initial events of the crisis took place before the Nativity of St Mary on 8 September, while John sets them after that date, and he seems to believe that the whole Dover incident actually took place in Canterbury, where Eustace landed, according to his account.

Joseph Stevenson, the mid-Victorian translator of what was then known as the *Chronicle of Florence of Worcester*,[5] further confused the issue by setting the incident and the castle at Dover, either because he mistranslated Doruuerniam as Dover, or more likely because he used the *Chronicle* to correct Florence/John's account. It seems unlikely that Eustace had enough men left to man a castle anywhere after the bloody Dover incident, and even if he had, there was no reason for them to remain in Kent as a target for the people of Dover, who were mobilising for an attack on them when they fled. Perhaps most significantly, the Canterbury annalist made no mention of Eustace's men establishing a castle in or around the city, or anywhere else in Kent, as he surely would have done if they had.

Since Robert's fortified residence in Essex cannot have been Osbern's castle, which we know from the *Chronicle* was somewhere in Herefordshire, we are left with the possibility that it was one of the castles specifically referred to in the *Chronicle* and Domesday: the castle possibly near Leominster in Herefordshire; the castle at Hereford; or the pre-Conquest castle at Ewyas Harold, Herefordshire. This was the starting point for the two Victorian scholars whose work has been most influential in relation to Osbern's castle; unfortunately so since they have succeeded in obscuring the true location and date of its construction for more than a century.

The battle for scholastic control of this uncharted territory began in the late 1860s, when Edward Augustus Freeman, scholar and distinguished fellow of Trinity College, Oxford and later Regius Professor of Modern History of that university, began to publish his ambitious five volume work (six with the index), *The History of The Norman Conquest of England*. Freeman had already published studies on federalism in ancient Greece, the English constitution and the history of the Saracens, and was regarded as an authority on English history in the eleventh and twelfth centuries. Though not now highly regarded as a source, Freeman had a determined band of champions in his day,[6] and indeed has continued to find admirers. Author Eric Linklater, whose *Conquest of England* marked the 900th anniversary of the Conquest in 1966, lauded Freeman's work in his bibliography. He was, said Linklater, 'invaluable', 'magisterial' and 'scrupulously careful to quote in very generous footnotes and long appendices the authorities on whom he built his narrative', though the author also admitted that 'his opinions

4 An 1886 portrait of E.A. Freeman, whose massive history of the Norman Conquest came in for a great deal of criticism, especially from J.H. Round.

may not all be so generally acceptable today as they were some ninety years ago'. This last was something of an understatement considering the ire that greeted Freeman's work in some quarters on its appearance.

In what was undoubtedly his major work, Freeman argued improbably that the Conquest had no real effect on the character or institutions of England, and startled contemporaries by proposing that the famous 1066 battlefield should be called 'Senlac' instead of 'Hastings', after the ridge on which Harold took his stand. That was ironic since the name that Freeman sought to attach to the site where his great hero, King Harold, fell was not the English name for the location, but a 'Normanization' of the Anglo-Saxon *sand-lacu*, meaning 'sandy brook'.[7] Many of Freeman's ideas were regarded as eccentric or idiosyncratic, and not surprisingly many of his conclusions have been upset, though in relation to pre-Conquest castles some of his ideas have surprisingly survived, not to say thrived, right up to the present day, as will be seen shortly.

Freeman and his massive history subsequently drew the academic fire of John Horace Round, Balliol scholar, rising star of medieval history and later one of the founders of, and major contributors to, the Victoria County History series, who became an implacable detractor of Freeman's work. Freeman was no stranger to controversy himself; he had severely damaged the reputation of successful historian J.A. Froude with largely unjust and vicious attacks on his *History of England*.[8] He also quarrelled bitterly with the editor of the *National Dictionary of Biography*, who refused to substitute Anglo-Saxon names, such as Eadweard and Eadgyth, for the more familiar Edward, Edith, and so on.[9] Even his biographer, who expressed warm regard for the professor, admitted he was a 'severe and somewhat harsh critic'.[10] Now Freeman was to learn how it felt to be on the receiving end of attacks from a scholar who more than matched his own aggression. As Round himself later said: '[Freeman] bitterly resented the treatment he meted out so freely to others being meted out, under any circumstances, to himself'.[11] Round is still thought of as a fine genealogist and a valuable pioneer of Domesday Book scholarship, but contemporaries nevertheless regarded him with some suspicion. Perhaps the most telling remarks on his character came from Henry Maxwell Lyte, deputy-keeper of the Public Record Office from 1886. The two men had collaborated closely on various projects, but after Round's death Lyte said he had always 'had an uncomfortable feeling' about him, 'founded upon incidents which cannot be mentioned in a biography', and he added, 'His extraordinary gifts were…marred by intense egotism and combativeness'.[12]

Round had been critical of the many errors in Freeman's largest work from the first, but respectfully so. However in 1882 Round published a history of Colchester Castle,[13] which Freeman made the mistake of criticising.

5 A portrait of J.H. Round *c.* 1900.

Round, according to his biographer, 'resented any criticism, particularly when couched in the patronising terms used by Freeman'.[14] Resentment of criticism was certainly a charge which could be levelled at both of these men. In 1884, the year in which Freeman became Regius professor, Round published the first of his furious attacks on Freeman's work in periodicals of the day. The two men had opposing party political loyalties and Round, who had independent means and no need of academic preferment, claimed Freeman's chair was a political appointment. Politics mixed with literature in the following year when Round launched a bitter attack on a pamphlet of Freeman's on the history of the House of Lords, and he followed this up with further attacks on Freeman's history of the Conquest. In 1886 Round published a series of three papers in *The Antiquary* under a general heading which mischievously ignored Freeman's professorial title: 'Is Mr Freeman accurate?' There was no doubt of his answer, as he tore into a series of 'errors' and 'inaccuracies' in *The Norman Conquest* with some relish. Freeman was apparently furious but avoided direct confrontation, preferring to let proteges tackle Round in articles and letters in various periodicals, while he fired off angry letters to friends and, it was claimed, tried to persuade the editor of the *Antiquarian Magazine*, another journal in which he had been criticised, to stop publishing Round's attacks on him.[15]

Even as late as 1895, when Round's most influential book, *Feudal England*, was published, he was still lambasting Freeman, three years after the professor's death.[16] Freeman stood accused, not to say convicted, of being 'a mere pedant' with scant regard for accuracy,[17] for frequently muddling different people of the same name, and, no doubt with an eye to Freeman's proposal for renaming the battlefield, Round quoted Macauley: '... ancient names, which he mangles in defiance both of custom and of reason'.[18] Round had to grudgingly admit that the Regius professor had been quite a live performer, but he nevertheless indicted him for 'that subtle commixture of guesswork and fact, which leaves us in doubt as to what is proved and what is merely hypothesis'.[19] In *Anglo-Saxon England*[20] Sir Frank Stenton attempted to defend Freeman against Round's charges of inaccuracy, but he nevertheless admitted: 'Much of the criticism to which his [Freeman's] work has given rise was caused by his reliance on evidence which will not bear a close examination'.

Many of the difficulties with Freeman's work arose from his careless working methods. Round's biographer said the professor 'wrote at high speed, often on several projects simultaneously, seldom revising his original drafts'.[21] So it was little wonder that his writings contained many inaccuracies. One instance of the problems with Freeman's work was the apparently persuasive rationale he offered for the 'invasion' of Herefordshire by Norman castle builders, when he discussed the fate of Swein Godwineson's lands

after the black sheep of Godwine's family left England in disgrace and went
to Denmark. Freeman was aware that the Abingdon annal for 1049, when
Swein returned to try to reclaim his lands, suggested that they had been
shared out between Harold Godwinson and Cnut and Godwine's Danish
nephew, Beorn, but despite this he suggested that Ralph, Edward's nephew,
who apparently did become earl of Hereford in late 1051 or 1052 after the
Godwinesons were exiled, also held the county for four years from 1046,[22]
even though Swein probably did not leave England until 1047.[23] If true,
this would suggest that Ralph might have built a castle in Hereford in 1047
or soon afterwards, though it doesn't explain why there was no mention
of such a castle in the chronicles. Freeman advanced no evidence for this
and his only argument was his previous assertion, for which he also had no
evidence, that the Normans had taken root in Herefordshire before 1051.[24]
This was simply piling one unsupported assertion on another, to produce a
conclusion which had no basis in fact or reasoning.

Though the evidence is not clear, and the details of Beorn's earldom
are unknown, the facts which exist suggest that Beorn held Herefordshire
during Swein's absence, if indeed anyone did, since it is perfectly possible
that Harold and Beorn held Swein's estates without holding his titles. In
1047 Godwine was still at something like the height of his powers, having
in the space of the previous four years obtained substantial earldoms for
his two eldest sons and married his eldest daughter to the king, and there
was little likelihood that he would allow lands which he had wrested
from Mercia to go out of his family's control. With his other sons not yet
old enough to succeed to the earldom or the estates, his Danish nephew
helped ensure that the lands remained within the family. It might be
argued that even without Ralph in control of Herefordshire, Normans
might have been given lands in the county, but the acrimony of Godwine's
relations with Robert of Jumieges made it inconceivable that he would
be prepared to create a power base for Robert's countrymen. If Harold
Godwineson had become earl over Herefordshire in 1047 he would have
been no more likely to hand the county back to Swein in 1050 than he
was in 1049, but Beorn had been murdered by Swein in 1049, leaving the
lands he held available for Swein on his final return. If Ralph had held
Herefordshire from his uncle, the king, since 1046 or 47, why would he
simply hand the county back to Swein in 1050? Freeman explained away
this problem by suggesting that Ralph had been given Worcestershire and
Warwickshire, the old kingdom of the Hwicca tribe in 1050, presumably in
place of Herefordshire.

Freeman's arguments, such as they were, have since been repeatedly
discredited by historians. In 1908 the Victoria County History of
Herefordshire[25] said it was unlikely that Ralph had been earl over

Herefordshire prior to late 1051, though he had probably held Worcestershire and Warwickshire from 1050, the year in which he first attested a charter as an earl. In 1989 historian Ann Williams, author of the only published review of Ralph's life and career, agreed, though she suggested that Ralph may have held another earldom from 1050 or earlier. She argued that Beorn had probably also held the earldom of the East Midlands, which may have passed to Ralph in 1050 or before.[26] This was a convincing argument since Godwine's power, and ability to prevent land being taken out of the hands of his family, was very different in 1050, after Swein's return, than it had been in 1047. It was clear though, in the view of all the historians who have looked at this question, that Ralph did not become earl over Herefordshire earlier than late 1051. Despite this, Freeman's unsupported and discredited assertion that a Norman colony had been established in Herefordshire in the 1040s, under the protection of the king's nephew as earl, has gone marching gaily on through history. It is hard to say why this might be so, but it may not have helped that Round actually supported Freeman in this, writing: 'Mr Freeman rightly called attention to "the firm root which the Normans had taken in Herefordshire before 1051".'[27] He, of course, offered no evidence for this.

Sir Frank Stenton, in mid-twentieth century, asserted that Normans were established in Herefordshire prior to Godwine's fall.[28] In 1985 R. Allen Brown agreed.[29] Professor Barlow, in 2002,[30] claimed that Normans were established in Herefordshire in or by 1050. None of these distinguished historians quoted any reference for this information, but it must surely have come from Freeman. In Herefordshire, six years before the Victoria County History of the county discredited Freeman's assertion, Rev A.T. Bannister, the vicar of the Herefordshire village of Ewyas Harold, wrote a history of his village in which he repeated Freeman's baseless and discredited assertion that Ralph had become earl of Hereford in 1046, and that a Norman colony had quickly grown up around him in the county.[31] He gave no reference, but this was also clearly based in good faith on Freeman, whose work he obviously knew. Perhaps because the vicar was a respected local history researcher, this has continued to be the accepted version of events in Herefordshire local history right up to the present day.

It was inevitable that Round would criticise Freeman over his suggested locations of pre-Conquest castles. In the second volume of his massive work, Freeman claimed he had discovered the site of Osbern's castle.[32] He pointed out a Domesday reference which suggested that the castle near Leominster in north Herefordshire, mentioned in the *Chronicle* in 1052, was likely to have been Richard's Castle, which has given its name to a village between Leominster and Ludlow. It was apparently built by Richard fitz Scrob, a Norman holding land there under Edward the Confessor, whose son Osbern held a wooden castle, Castle Avretone, there at the time of Domesday garrisoned with 23 men. Freeman's argument for identification of this as Osbern's castle was simple: 'Pentecost ... is the same as Osbern, the son of Richard of Richard's Castle'.[33] He advanced no evidence, nor even argument for this claim. Even putting aside the fact – which must surely have been known to Freeman – that Osbern was a common Norman name at that time, this always seemed unlikely, since the castle was and is known by Richard's name, not Osbern's.

Round responded with a scathing attack which must have appeared originally amongst his vast output of magazine articles, and was included in his book, *Feudal England* in 1895. 'This assumption is not only baseless,' he said, 'but also most improbable'. He pointed out that the Osbern of Richard's Castle did not surrender his castle in 1052 and was later seen to be holding both land and office in the county.[34] A few years later Round was supported by the Victoria County History of Herefordshire,[35] which suggested that Osbern fitz Richard was definitely holding office in the county in 1060, 'probably as sheriff'. Osbern, son of Richard, was in fact shown by Domesday to be a major English landowner, as Freeman well knew. 'We have here,' wrote Round, 'one of those cases characteristic of the Professor's work, in which he first formed an idea, and then, under its spell, fitted the facts to it without question ... The whole of this history is sheer assumption, based on confusion alone.'

Round insisted that there were actually four pre-Conquest castles, one of which was indeed that identified by Freeman at Richard's Castle although his identification of it as Osbern's castle was mistaken. The other sites on Round's list were Robert fitz Wymarc's 'castle' at Clavering in Essex,[36] which he couldn't resist pointing out that Freeman had been unable to find; a castle built by Ralph of Mantes at Hereford; and the pre-Conquest castle at Ewyas Harold. Round argued that the last of these, the castle at Ewyas Harold, was the true castle held by Osbern Pentecost. None of these castles had been proven to exist through physical evidence, but the 1908 Victoria County History of Herefordshire, to which Round contributed, supported his theories,[37] and they have since been generally accepted by such distinguished historians as R. Allen Brown[38] and Sir Frank Stenton,[39] who wrote a foreword to the last edition of *Feudal England*, which appeared as recently as 1964.

In 1934 Sir Frank referred to Osbern's second castle, for which no site had been identified, in one of the Herefordshire volumes of the Royal Commission on Historical Monuments,[40] but, putting aside references in *Anglo-Saxon England,* it does not appear to have been until 1968 that any major historian extracted the full detail on castles from the chronicles, when distinguished castle historian Dr Derek Renn published his book *Norman*

Castles in Britain. Having reviewed the *Chronicle* material, Dr Renn suggested, without either evidence or even argument, that the first castle must have been at Hereford.[41] In the following year R. Allen Brown published his book *The Normans and the Norman Conquest*. Though he still stuck rigidly to those sites identified by Round, he also muddied the already distinctly opaque waters by suggesting that Osbern's castle was at Hereford.[42] Again he offered no evidence and this proposal seemed to defy the logic of his own argument, since he suggested that Ralph may not have become earl of Hereford until 1053, when the *Chronicle* made clear that the castle, likely to have been built by Ralph, dated from 1051. Why the site would be regarded as Osbern's castle if it was built by Ralph was something of a mystery, which the professor didn't seek to solve. Neither of these distinguished historians attempted to review the work by Freeman and Round, which continued to form the basis of modern thinking about England's first castle. Thus despite the fiercely competitive haste in which their conclusions were reached, there appears to have been no previous review of Freeman and Round's work since it was written more than a century ago.

Which, if any, of these castles was built by Osbern? Clearly not Robert's castle, which was not in Herefordshire and was referred to separately from Osbern's castle in the *Chronicle*. Hereford seems an improbable choice, since it would undoubtedly have been built by Ralph, not Osbern, and since, as we have seen, there is no evidence that Ralph became earl over Herefordshire before at least late 1051, it has to be ruled out since Osbern's castle had, said the chroniclers, been built by early September in that year. Freeman's identification of Richard's Castle as a pre-Conquest castle has been generally accepted, but even if his identification of it as Osbern's castle had not been discredited by Round, it would now be ruled out since later historians, such as Stenton,[43] seem satisfied that Richard did not establish himself in Herefordshire until 1052, having perhaps come to England first when William of Normandy visited Edward in late 1051. This leaves Ewyas Harold, the site which Round suggested was Osbern's castle, and which has been accepted as such by historians for more than a century. But what evidence is there for Round's claim?

Round's original claim was again likely to have appeared amongst his many magazine articles at an earlier date, but was included in his book *Feudal England* in 1895. He advanced three arguments, two of which were actually worthless in supporting his claim. The first was the Domesday reference to the castle at Ewyas Harold being re-fortified after the Conquest, which suggested that it must be a pre-Conquest castle, but did not prove that it was Osbern's castle. 'Ewyas Harold fits in also,' said Round, 'with the chronicle's mention [in 1052] of the Normans fleeing "west" to Pentecost's castle,' but again this does little for his case, since we don't know where the Normans were fleeing from, and even if we assumed London, 'somewhere west of London' would cover a lot of territory. His third argument, and that on which his whole case must rest, is based on Domesday. The key part of the Domesday entry relating to Ewyas Harold read:

> Alfred of Marlborough holds the castle of Ewyas [Harold] from King William. The king himself granted him the lands which Earl William [fitz Osbern], who had refortified the castle, had given him.

Alfred was a major landowner who held lands in many English counties and was obviously regarded by the king as trustworthy enough to be given control of an important strategic fortress on the Welsh border. The Domesday commissioners, who collected the information, frequently also listed the holder of the land *TRE* (*Tempore Regis Edwardi*), roughly 'in the time of king Edward', and it would have saved us all a great deal of trouble had they done so on this occasion. However, as Round pointed out, the commissioners appended a note to the entries immediately following, for the Herefordshire manors of Burghill and Brinsop, a few miles west of Hereford and some distance from Ewyas Harold but also held by Alfred:

> Osbern uncle of Alfred held these two manors *TRE* when Godwine and Harold had been exiled.

Osbern, as we have noted, was a common Norman name at the time, but the presence of this Osbern as a landowner in Herefordshire during 1051-2 strongly suggested that he was the Osbern referred to in the chronicles. Round, in other respects a sound if pugnacious scholar, made a cursory, almost casual case in support of his identification of Ewyas Harold as Osbern Pentecost's castle,[44] as if he felt that having disposed of Freeman's argument with respect to Richard's Castle he had little else to prove. Having identified a pre-Conquest castle and an Osbern with a later family connection to it, he simply assumed that the castle at Ewyas Harold must have been Osbern's castle referred to in the *Chronicle*. Round's claim was subsequently supported by the Victoria County History of Herefordshire,[45] and has never been challenged or seriously reviewed since 1895, which is unfortunate, since there are good reasons for believing that it was totally wrong.

Osbern is shown in Domesday as the *TRE* holder only of the manors of Burghill and Brinsop, not of Ewyas Harold or its castle, for which no *TRE* holder is listed. The entry in Domesday referring to lands held by Alfred of Marlborough is generally detailed and informative, relating a number of changes in land ownership dating back over the previous 35 years. Given the detail there it makes no sense to assume that Osbern also held other lands in addition to Burghill and Brinsop but the commissioner forgot or didn't think it was necessary to mention the fact. Herefordshire researcher Bruce Coplestone-Crow[46] has suggested that there was a dispute over ownership of these manors between Alfred and landowner Bernard de Neufmarche, which may explain why Alfred was keen to draw the attention of the commissioners to his uncle's ownership, and thus his prior claim to them, but this does not prove that Osbern held Ewyas Harold. The points above alone cast doubt on Round's casual claim but there are further facts which entirely invalidate it. Though the *Chronicle* was not precise in its location of Osbern's castle, the chronicler was very clear that it was 'in Herefordshire, in Earl Swein's territory', and there is good reason to believe that Round's chosen location, at Ewyas Harold, was not in Herefordshire or in the earl's territory at that time, and that Round knew that. To look more closely at Round's flawed theory we will need to delve into the murky depths of the pre-Conquest political geography of the troubled English border with Wales.

Herefordshire had always stood as the English sentinel on the border with Wales, and if raiders from the west were a common feature of life along its western boundary, then so were invaders from the east. As early as the late sixth century, said a later Welsh monastic writer at Llandaff,[47] the Anglo-Saxon invaders were pressing across the border:

… great tribulations and plunderings were committed by the most treacherous Saxon nation, and principally on the borders of Wales and England towards Hereford, so that all the border country of Wales was nearly destroyed, and especially about the River Wye.

This account seemed to point to the invaders occupying the land between the Wye and the little River Dore,[48] which runs through the Golden Valley, at the head of which stands Ewyas Harold. The village commands what in times past would have been an important gap route from south Wales into Herefordshire, where the A465 Swansea to Hereford road crosses the B4347 Monmouth to Hay-on-Wye road. The valley was apparently named through an etymological accident. The Celts named the Dore, their word *dubra* meaning 'stream'. It was rendered into old Welsh as *istratour* which meant 'valley of the stream', but *our* also meant 'gold', hence the Golden Valley. After a time peace was restored and land was returned to its owners, but much of the area had largely been depopulated by the invaders or by 'an uncommon pestilence' which the invaders doubtless brought with them, and to which the Welsh will have had no immunity. Depopulation of the border area was to be a common theme in the centuries that followed.

In a pattern that had no doubt continued sporadically during the intervening period, there was raiding from both sides before and during the early years of the reign of Offa of Mercia. In 743 the *Chronicle* recorded that Aethelbald, then the king of Mercia, campaigned against the Welsh, backed by Cuthred of Wessex. The Welsh retaliated with destruction in the Hereford area in 745 and the devastation of the town in 760. Mercia in Offa's day stretched from the Trent and Mersey to the Thames Valley, and from Wales to the Fens, so the whole of the Welsh border was in his dominion, but it was from the central area of Powys that the main threat came, as the Welsh tried to recover some of the land they had previously lost in Mercian incursions.

Offa fought back with incursions into Wales in 777 and 783, and it was probably in 785 that he began building on the western boundary of Mercia the great dyke which bears his name, though its existence was not recorded until a century later, in Asser's *Life of King Alfred*,[49] and much about it is still uncertain. It has however attracted a good deal of archaeological interest. Offa's Dyke consisted of an earth bank thirty feet (10m) wide with a ditch six feet (2m) deep and 12ft (4m) wide, and aside from making absolutely clear to raiders that they were entering Mercia, it would have formed a formidable barrier to them crossing and would have made it impossible to drive stolen livestock back into Wales. Asser, a Welshman by birth, said it sat 'between Mercia and Wales, from sea to sea', and sections of dyke do exist between Sedbury Cliffs on the Severn near Chepstow and Prestatyn in north Wales, but archaeologists are satisfied that the original dyke was only 64 miles long, between Rushock Hill on the north side of the Herefordshire plain and Llanfynydd, near Mold in Clwyd,[50] though it may have been added to before Asser recorded it.

In Herefordshire, to the south of Rushock Hill, the dyke was apparently later and discontinuous, leading down to the River Wye at Bridge Sollers, a few miles west of Hereford, after which the Wye formed the Mercian boundary throughout the remainder of the county. In many areas the dyke still follows the line of the boundary between England and Wales as it is today, but this is not true of Herefordshire. The county now takes in a large area beyond the Wye, bounded by Hay-on-Wye and the Brecon Beacons National Park on the west and stretching almost to Monmouth in the south. This part of modern-day Herefordshire is testament to the expansionist ambitions of the marcher earls, but was clearly not English territory in Offa's day, nor in the centuries that followed, so there may have been little, if any, of this land which formed part of the earldom of Herefordshire in 1051.

There is no source from 1051 which gives detailed information about the state of the border at that time, but there is a good deal of information available from 1086. Domesday showed that immediately beyond the Wye to the south lay the Welsh or Anglo-Welsh district of Archenfield, a liberty

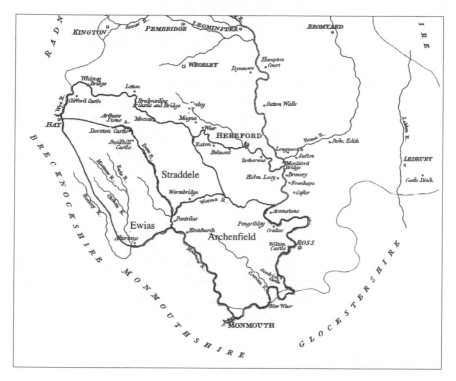

6 The districts beyond the River Wye as they may have been in 1051, drawn on a county map of 1804. Archenfield was a liberty under the Crown. Straddele, to the east of the River Dore, was apparently Welsh though there was English land ownership there. Ewias was a Welsh lordship, still in Welsh hands in 1086 though its chief settlement, later to become Ewyas Harold, came into English possession between 1055 and 1065.

under the crown from times past, that is, it enjoyed special privileges in return for loyalty to the king, though this may not have been part of the domain of the earl over Herefordshire before the Conquest. To the north of Archenfield lay Straddele, a Welsh inhabited area taking in the eastern side of today's Golden Valley. Though Straddele was Welsh, there had been some English land ownership there for some time, though this expansion was not one-sided; in the tenth and eleventh centuries up to a dozen estates in Herefordshire were held by Welsh princes.[51] In 1086 the Domesday commissioners found that some landholdings in Straddele were reckoned in the usual English measure of hides, and were equal to roughly 120 acres, though even by that date they found that little west of the River Dore was in English hands.[52] Where the Normans found measures in hides they invariably used them, as they did in this area; only where land had not previously been under English control did they go to the trouble of reckoning it in the old Danish measure of carucates. Though some parts of Straddele appeared to be well settled by English landowners, again it may not have been part of Herefordshire prior to the Conquest. Further west, encompassing the land between the River Dore and the Black Mountains, lay the ancient Welsh cantref of Ewias, of which Round himself suggested,[53] Ewyas Harold, or Ewias as it was then known, 'was the head'.

Twelfth-century writer Gerald of Wales explained that a cantref was 'a word made up from *cant* meaning hundred and *tref* meaning vill … a term used in both Welsh and Irish for a stretch of land which contains a hundred vills,'[54] a vill being an area of land which was the smallest unit used in local administration. Modern Welsh historian Roger Turvey explained that cantrefs 'were lordships, territories which commanded the patriotic loyalty of their inhabitants'.[55] Thus the cantref of Ewias, with the settlement of Ewias as its most important settlement, was an ancient Welsh lordship. But had it been so in 1051? Even Round seemed to agree that it had. In his Domesday commentary in the Victoria County History of Herefordshire he noted that 'Ewyas Harold is reckoned in "carucates" like the recent conquests from the Welsh' rather than hidated which indicated 'an ancient English possession', and the district of Ewias 'remained even in 1086 economically as well as ecclesiastically Welsh, while even politically its conquest was probably still imperfect'.[56] Thus, though he was the foremost Domesday scholar of his day, Round took no account of the position of Ewias as a pre-Conquest Welsh lordship in making his identification of Ewyas Harold as the site of Osbern Pentecost's castle, though his work showed he was well aware of it.

Other writers have since agreed with this view. In 1954 it was noted, 'Ewias is an ancient Welsh territorial name, and Domesday Book records so little of it that it must still have been largely in Welsh hands'.[57] In 1983 the editors of Herefordshire Domesday agreed that Ewias was 'on the point of being acquired by the Normans' in 1086. They pointed out that: 'Ewyas Harold Castle [was] built on unhidated land probably gained from the Welsh under King Edward the Confessor', and suggested that the re-fortified castle was being used in 1086 as a base for the conquest of Ewias.[58]

By the time of Domesday, after vigorous campaigning in the border area by William fitz Osbern, the first post-Conquest Norman earl over Herefordshire, both Archenfield and Straddele were included in the earldom and the county, but Ewias had not been conquered, so clearly it must have been outside Herefordshire in 1051, and there is evidence to support this. In 1055 a force of Welsh, Viking and Mercian raiders, who had sacked Hereford, were pursued by Harold Godwineson. John of Worcester described how Harold 'boldly invaded the Welsh borders … encamped beyond Straddele'. This clearly suggests that Straddele was within the Welsh borders and is confirmed by the *Chronicle*: 'Harold … went a little way into Wales' and 'pitched his camp at "Straddele" within the Welsh borders.' This confirmed that Ewias, beyond Straddele, was undoubtedly Welsh territory at the time that Harold encamped his army below the Black Mountains in 1055.

It would seem though, that Ewias, later Ewyas Harold, the chief settlement of the Welsh lordship of Ewias, must have been taken out of Welsh control some time before 1066, since the castle there was built prior to the Conquest. Herefordshire researcher Bruce Coplestone-Crow has noted the existence of two English settlements at Ewyas Harold, named Manitune and Mulstonestone,[59] which he dated from before 1066, though how much earlier than 1066 is not clear. With no evidence of land ownership in the area to help us, it is necessary to look at border politics to determine when Ewyas Harold may have been taken out of Welsh hands, and from this point of view, there is no record, evidence or likelihood of English expansion on the border at any time in the eleventh century until the late 1050s.

Despite a very full *Chronicle* record of Aethelred's reign, there is no evidence and little likelihood of any English expansion on the Welsh border whilst England was beset by Viking raids. According to the *Encomium*, Cnut claimed hegemony over Wales, but this was likely to have been a simple matter of the Welsh princes accepting his overlordship, as they had done in previous centuries with other rulers, including Offa and Alfred, since he was far more interested in securing his northern empire than expansion to the west. The earldom covering Herefordshire was one of three created out of former Mercian lands in the early years of Cnut's reign, but there is no record of it having been bestowed on anyone until Swein Godwinson received it as part of his lands, probably in 1043, which strongly suggested that the border was quiet throughout the intervening period. On this border 'quiet' never meant free from tension, and in 1039 Leofric's brother Edwin was killed in an ambush, along with many of his men, when he was unwise enough to venture into Wales. Understandably there were no further Mercian incursions. Swein had substantial lands aside from Herefordshire, and his only recorded action on the border was his interference in Welsh politics in 1046, which probably prompted the Welsh raids of 1049 and 1052, but it was not until after the sacking of Hereford in 1055 that there was any major response from the English side.

Harold Godwineson's arrival on the border with an army in 1055, and his accession to the earldom, either in that year or after December 1057, was undoubtedly a turning point for English expansion on the border. It is very likely that in the next few years Harold vigorously expanded the western border of his new possession. Domesday showed that Harold was the holder *TRE* of lands in both Straddele and Archenfield; for example, the Straddele manors of Monnington and Bredwardine in the Domesday record of Alfred of Marlborough's holdings were both held *TRE* by Harold, along with four other manors in Bacton and Howton, Dorstone and Middlewood and six manors in Archenfield comprising lands in Pontrilas, Old Radnor, 'Mateurdin' and Chickward. It is perhaps notable that in each district some manors are hidated but most notable is that no *TRE* value is given for any of Harold's 12 manors in these two districts, and most are either described as waste *TRE* or no information is given, which may suggest he had little time after obtaining this land to organise its use. When Harold acquired these holdings we do not know, but it is notable that the further north and west you go in the present-day county beyond the Wye the more likely you are to bump into his holdings, and most probably he began putting pressure on the border from the time he attained the earldom or before, culminating in his harrying of Wales in 1062-3 which resulted in the killing of Gruffyd ap Llewlleyn by his own people. Interestingly, three Welsh landholdings, at Llanvair Discoed, Dinham and Portskewett, all now in Monmouthshire, were reckoned in Gloucestershire Domesday, but this territory remained in Welsh hands until Harold annexed it to Herefordshire in the 1060s.[60] Clearly there was tension even then. A hunting lodge Harold was having built for the king in the last of these manors was destroyed and the workmen killed by the Welsh in 1065.

Given that there is no previous record, evidence or likelihood of English expansion on the border for some decades prior to Harold's arrival, it can only have been after 1055 that Ewyas Harold was taken out of Welsh hands, but that expansion would have come too late for Osbern. Why he chose to build his castle is yet to be determined, but it is inconceivable that he would have tried to build it within a Welsh lordship in a troubled border area, half a day's ride beyond the border, where it would have been resented and vulnerable to Welsh attack. Ewyas Harold was clearly a strategic site, ideally suited to border defence, but well beyond the border at that time, and needing the resources of an earl or major landowner to command the labour needed for its construction. Osbern had no such resources and was unlikely to have gained support from the local inhabitants, even assuming he could surmount the problems of a group of French speakers trying to tell an uncooperative group of Welsh speakers what they wanted them to do. Most importantly, the *Chronicle* made clear that Osbern's castle was in Herefordshire, and Ewyas Harold clearly was not in Herefordshire in 1051, therefore it cannot have been the site of Osbern's castle. Because of Round's reputation as a scholar however, historians have continued to support his baseless theory.

Clearly Osbern's castle was the first to be built in England, not only because it was the first to be identified by the chroniclers, but because none of the other castles built in the period 1051-2 could have been built as early as September 1051, when Osbern's castle was in existence. But if none of the locations identified by the *Chronicle* or Domesday could have been the site of Osbern's castle, where was it? For that matter, who was he, and why did he build his castle? To find answers to these questions we need to return to the point at which the chronicler first revealed the existence of Osbern's castle, in early September 1051, when England had been plunged into crisis and was on the verge of civil war.

Chapter Seven

The First Castle

The *Chronicle* made clear that the existence of the first Norman castle in England was revealed when events in the political crisis of late 1051 were developing fast. Incensed by Godwine's refusal to act against Kent, the king had ominously called his council to meet seven days later on 8 September at Gloucester, where he was holding court. This clearly put Godwine's initial acrimonious meeting with the king on 1 September. Since he will have been well aware that he could be outlawed by the council, he and his sons responded determinedly by gathering men from their shires and assembling an army in Gloucestershire to put pressure on the king. Though Edward may well have plotted to create this crisis, he was clearly taken aback by the unexpected violence of Godwine's response.

It was when Godwine presented his ultimatum that he complained of 'the Frenchmen in the castle'. The date at which that happened was not stated but was probably not earlier than 7/8 September, since his ultimatum was appealing diplomatically for the advice of the king and the council, and Leofric and Siward, the key members of the council aside from Godwine and his sons, had to travel from Mercia and Northumbria, and cannot have arrived earlier than that. The apparent difference between the diplomatic language of the ultimatum and the curt demand for handing over the castle's occupants, and the confusion of the various chroniclers over the castle, may suggest that it was a late addition to the ultimatum. As was shown in Chapter Six, many historians would wish to claim that this castle could have been built some time before these events, but there is no evidence to support this view, and it is inconceivable that Godwine would have allowed Normans to colonise lands controlled by his family. It is also worth remembering that the one detailed contemporary source we have, the Canterbury annalist, wrote the castle was built 'at this time'. This is a vague phrase and it could be argued that 'at this time' could refer to a period of months, a season, a year, or even a decade, but that would very much depend on the context in which it was being used. Here it is being used in an almost day-to-day description of fast-moving events, which suggests that the phrase was meant to be taken literally. It therefore seems fairly safe to say that this castle could not have been built very much earlier than September 1051, yet on 8 September it was in existence. How and why can that have happened?

We have seen that Godwine probably knew of the incident at Dover a week before the beginning of September, and may well have considered at least the possibility that Edward had some plot afoot to disadvantage him. If so, he and his sons may well have begun to call out armed men from their lands in the last days of August. With Edward at Gloucester, and his nephew Ralph, the Godwinesons neighbour, as earl of Worcestershire and part of Warwickshire, it is inconceivable that they will not have known of this. The men of Herefordshire must have been amongst the first to assemble in Gloucestershire, since they could have covered the 30 miles from Hereford to Gloucester in a day. This was significant because the absence of armed men from the county will have left the border with Wales defenceless. It was only two years earlier that a Welsh army had joined with Irish pirates to cross the border and raid Herefordshire, largely wiping out a scratch force put together by Bishop Ealdred of Worcester, and no doubt the border area remained tense, with the people of Herefordshire fearing further raids. If the Welsh took advantage of the political crisis to raid across the border while it was left defenceless, the consequences for Herefordshire could have been devastating. In the circumstances there would have been an urgent need for a stronghold to try to defend the border, but why should Osbern care about border defence or the fate of Herefordshire? To answer that question we need to look at who he was and what he was likely to have been doing in England at that time.

Nothing has previously been known about Osbern, but by tracing the antecedents of Alfred of Marlborough, a major landowner under William I, who was shown by Domesday to have been Osbern's nephew, it has been possible to discover his origins. Osbern came from Le Beny-Bocage near Vire, in the south of the Calvados area of Lower Normandy, in the Pays du Bocage region of the Cotentin or Cherbourg peninsula. The peninsula had traditionally been inhabited by Bretons, but it was either granted to Normandy or annexed to it by Duke William Longsword, son of Hrolfr, the founder of the duchy, in 933. Osbern's family name was Malbenc and he was probably one of at least three brothers. Alfred's father, Guillame Malbenc, born about 1020, must have been the eldest since French tradition records that he succeeded to the lordship of Le Beny-Bocage. Usually the next in line would enter the church, and Alfred apparently had an association with the abbot of the nearby abbey of Mont St Michel,[1] who may have been another uncle.

Guillame had at least two and possibly three sons, probably born after 1040. Alfred, whose apparently English name probably came from nearby Brittany, where it had long been popular,[2] may have been the eldest since he succeeded to his father's lordship, but he also held modest estates at Pembridge, Herefordshire, and Severn Stoke, Worcestershire, before the Conquest,[3] though this must have been well after his uncle Osbern was in Herefordshire, since Alfred was probably only 11 or 12 years old in 1051. It has been speculatively suggested that Alfred was an equerry to Edward the Confessor,[4] and he certainly may have held some office under William since he had substantial estates in England after 1066, holding 281 hides in Herefordshire, Worcestershire, Wiltshire, Somerset, Hampshire and Surrey, but he apparently divided his time between England and Normandy, since he witnessed a series of charters in the duchy between around 1069 and 1081.[5]

Guillame was probably at Hastings with Duke William, and after the Conquest he received the barony of Nantwich in Cheshire, which subsequently passed to another son, William, Alfred's younger brother, about 1070. The genealogy of Guillame Malbenc's family in the 1580 Visitation of Cheshire,[6] though somewhat confused, referred to another son named Hugo, making it very likely that Osbern's companion in 1052, mentioned in John of Worcester's chronicle, was another of his nephews. It should be added that some confusion has arisen over the identification of Osbern's companion, because Victorian translations of the *Chronicle* of Florence of Worcester, such as that of Joseph Stevenson in 1853,[7] 'Anglicized' his name as Hugh, but the latest, impeccably researched version of the *Chronicle* of John of Worcester, gives his name as Hugo. Osbern's nickname, 'Pentecost', has never been explained and remains something of a mystery. Such names invariably had a humorous, often cruelly satirical element related to the recipient's character, but in this case there is no such obvious meaning. The name may have been corrupted in its translation from Old French, or Osbern may have had some connection to the Christian festival of Pentecost, 50 days after Easter Sunday, which celebrates the coming of the Holy Spirit to the followers of Jesus 50 days after the resurrection. Perhaps he was born at Pentecost, or perhaps some aspect of the festival may have had a significance to contemporaries which is lost to us. Equally, Osbern's byname may not be as mysterious as it first appears. The *Oxford Dictionary of English Christian Names* shows that Pentecost was used as a forename in England from the thirteenth to seventeenth centuries, and it may perhaps have been used earlier than that in Europe, so Pentecost could simply be another fore- or baptismal name.

As a younger brother, Osbern would have been expected to make his own way in the world. This was by no means unusual. Younger sons of noble Norman families had long gone out across Europe and beyond, seeking their fortunes, usually by the sword, since it was for warfare that their training had fitted them. R. Allen Brown noted that in 1066 Normandy was full of knights, 'and had indeed been "exporting" them, especially as younger sons, for over a generation – to Spain, Italy and beyond'.[8] This was typical of the wandering Scandinavian roots from which the Normans had sprung, but with a veneer of Frankish knightly service to add respectability. Normans exiled from Normandy were frequently in demand, such as Rodulf, exiled by Emma's brother, Duke Richard II, who was urged by Pope Benedict to assist the Lombards, who were rebelling against Greek rule.[9] By the mid-eleventh century Normandy had become a 'rent-a-knight' agency, able to fulfil the needs of any wealthy client seeking to buy in the militarily trained and skilled. The knight, said the authors of a recent book on this Norman elite, 'exemplified the highest standards of military prowess. His instruction would begin as a mere boy. Future training included everything for a martial life: horsemanship, sword fighting, using the lance, rules of war, dress and etiquette'.[10]

Osbern, like Ralph of Mantes, was doubtless a younger son who had come to England, probably in his early twenties, to make his fortune, but unlike Ralph he had no well-placed relative to offer him advancement, since the chroniclers' ignorance of his name in September 1051, when the existence of his castle was revealed, showed he was not known at court or as a wealthy landowner. Certainly he could not remain in England without offering his service to a lord, and Ralph of Mantes would seem an obvious choice as someone to whom Osbern might offer service, since he had probably succeeded to the earldom of Worcestershire and Warwickshire in 1050 and would need good French knights. Ralph had good reason to be interested in the defence of the Herefordshire border. If the king was plotting the downfall of the Godwinesons, he was likely to have given some thought to who would replace Swein Godwineson in this important border area, and his trusted nephew Ralph, already holding an adjacent earldom, was the clear choice. But if the Welsh came across the border while the fighting men of the county were away in Gloucestershire, then Ralph would inherit nothing but a smoking ruin, which suggests that when the Herefordshire militia had been called out to Gloucestershire, he had an urgent need to send in men who could secure the border as quickly as possible, probably before the end of August. So far this is speculation, based on the facts that we have, but nothing more than circumstantial evidence. However, as we will see shortly, there is firm evidence which supports the view that Osbern was sent into Herefordshire to guard the border against Welsh attack.

If Ralph was Osbern's lord, which seems very likely to have been the case, then the force Osbern led into Herefordshire would have been made up of Ralph's personal military retainers, no doubt Normans seeking advancement like Osbern, and it was unlikely to have been a large force, since the military confrontation in Gloucestershire will have dictated that as few men as possible be removed from the king's forces. As a Norman knight this would not necessarily concern Osbern: William fitz Osbern – no relation – who became the first post-Conquest lord over Herefordshire, set out on one occasion to campaign in Flanders with only 10 men.[11] Osbern's men would be professional soldiers, they would be mounted, and they could move quickly to take up position in Herefordshire. But what position? There is no record of the circumstances of Osbern's 'invasion' of Herefordshire, so we need to put ourselves in his position, and consider where we would position ourselves with a small force to try to defend England from a Welsh force numbered in the hundreds at least. The obvious position to take up would be on the Wye, doubtless still the border at that time. Any military commander would realise that it was at the river crossing that the raiders would be at their most vulnerable, and the crossing closest to Hereford, the largest and wealthiest town in the county, would clearly be the defensive point to choose. Today a military commander would doubtless choose the point where the A465 road runs into Hereford from south Wales, but that would not have been Osbern's choice, because the road system then was very different.

The Anglo-Saxons excelled in many things, but they were not great builders, and most importantly, they were not road builders. In the eleventh century the English were still using the road system that the Romans had left behind more than 600 years earlier, and the main Roman road did not go to Hereford, an Anglo-Saxon settlement which did not exist in Roman times. The main north–south Roman route through Herefordshire, referred to as Watling Street, which ran from Wroxeter through the county to Carleon, ran by the Roman town of Magna, a few miles west of Hereford, and crossed the river, probably by a ford or causeway, around The Old Weir at Swainshill,[12] where an ancient weir still existed in the nineteenth century. This route, which is shown on Ordnance Survey maps, has been traced to the edge of the Golden Valley,[13] and possibly as far as Abbey Dore, site of a monastic settlement in the valley,[14] but probably ran on past Ewyas Harold to Abergavenny, the Roman town of Gobannium, one of the destinations of the road shown in the Antonine Itinerary. This had doubtless been the best route from Usk to Wye from ancient times, and it was still very much in use in the eleventh century.

Once the invaders approached the Wye near Hereford they had three likely alternative points at which to ford the river. There was a ford at Hereford, which gave the town its name, but it was too exposed to attack from the townsfolk, and the eastern ford, near the village of Hoarwithy,[15] was too far away to be worth bothering with. So the ford at Swainshill, on the line of

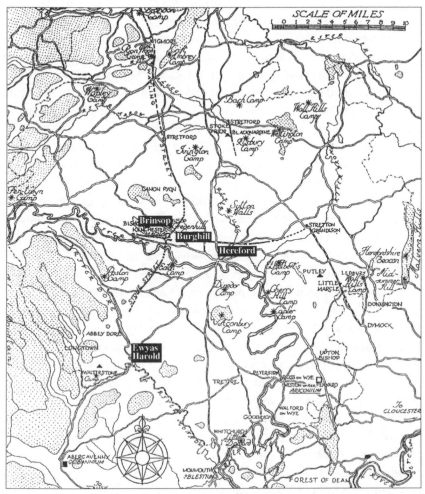

7 Osbern's manors of Burghill and Brinsop in relation to the River Wye and main north–
south Roman road through Herefordshire in the eleventh century. Also shown is Ewyas
Harold, the site Round claimed for Osbern's castle.

the main Roman road, was the obvious route to take. From the northern
side of the ford another Roman road ran around the city of Hereford to the
north. Clearly the Welsh did not always take this route into England. In 1049,
with 36 Viking ships at their disposal, they must have sailed around into the
Severn estuary and up to the Forest of Dean before raiding across country
into the extreme south of Herefordshire below Ross-on-Wye, and in 1052,
when the Anglo-Saxons and 'the Frenchmen from the castle' unsuccessfully
gave battle to the raiders near Leominster, it is possible that the incursion
was made direct into the north of the county. In 1055 however, when the
Welsh were part of a combined force with Vikings and rebel Mercians, it is
likely that they took the most direct route to Hereford, since the advancing

force met and defeated a probably inferior force of defenders a short distance from the town, before pillaging and burning it. On this evidence it seems clear that when the Welsh felt they had superiority, as was probably the case in 1055 and would certainly have been the case in September 1051 when the county was left defenceless, the easiest and most direct route into the county, which quickly brought raiders within striking distance of the prosperous county town, would have been the preferred route.

If Osbern set up his base immediately to the north of the ford he would be in a position commanding entry to the county and access to Hereford. At this point, even with only a few men, Osbern could hold off the Welsh, at least for a time, since the raiders would probably have been forced to cross in single file, which would make them vulnerable to attack by crossbowmen on the northern bank of the river. There is no chronicle record to show that Osbern did take up a defensive position on the River Wye, but there is evidence to support this view, and it is compelling. If we look back at Domesday, we see that the two manors that Osbern held in Herefordshire – the only English landholdings with which there is any evidence to connect Osbern – were the manors of Burghill and Brinsop, which maps of Herefordshire confirm to be the manors positioned either side of the ford by which the main eleventh-century route from Wales entered Herefordshire. This is surely too significant to be a mere coincidence. The positioning of the only two manors which we know Osbern held seems to be clear evidence that his task in Herefordshire was to protect the vital river crossing from Welsh incursions. Even if we assume that he was not serving Ralph and his arrival was not occasioned by the political crisis, the positioning of these two manors on this vital crossing must surely suggest that Osbern's task there was to hold a defensive position, and it is difficult to see what his motive for doing so might have been unless he was under orders from some senior figure at Edward's court. Ralph is the obvious choice since he is likely to have employed Norman knights, and he succeeded to the earldom over Herefordshire after the Godwinesons were exiled.

The position would be the best that Osbern could choose, but even with the defensive advantage it would give him, he could not hope to fight off a large force of Welshmen indefinitely. He could fight a rearguard action while riders were sent for reinforcements, but sooner or later numbers would tell and Osbern would inevitably be forced back away from the ford and would then need a final redoubt – he would need a castle. But where? Again, we need to look at the possibilities from Osbern's trained military viewpoint. Flat river meadows surround the ford and any stronghold there would be quickly overwhelmed; Osbern would have needed to be on higher ground. He needed to position his castle to the east of the ford, between the raiders and the city, and ideally he needed a site which already had some defensive works, which he could quickly refortify, since he had little time to get ready when the Welsh might turn up at any moment. Around a mile from the ford, and between three and four miles from Hereford, there was an ideal site, which would meet all these requirements, in the village of Burghill. The largest of the two manors that we know Osbern held, Burghill, as the name implies, stands on higher ground, above the Roman road leading into Hereford from the nearby ford. The *burg* element of the name strongly suggests that it was an Anglo-Saxon *burh*, or fortified settlement. There is a long tradition in the village that the area to the west of the church was once the site of Anglo-Saxon fortifications or earthworks,[16] and the Anglo-Saxon village name, given as Burgelle in Domesday, means 'hill of the fort'.[17] The modern village, much of which dates from the eighteenth and nineteenth centuries, has moved a little way down the hillside, but the Anglo-Saxon settlement must have been on higher ground, where the substantial parish church stands. The site to the west of the church, identified by tradition as the fortified settlement of Anglo-Saxon times, has a commanding position and though Osbern may have found its defences fallen into disrepair in the 35 relatively peaceful years since the end of Aethelred's reign, it would doubtless have had ditch and bank earthworks, and thus could be brought back into use fairly quickly. The Canterbury chronicler's no doubt exaggerated claim that Osbern's men 'inflicted all the injuries and insults they possibly could upon the king's men in that region', was almost certainly the result of Osbern's men demanding supplies from the villagers and forcing them to work on the refortification of the defensive works which would form Osbern's last line of defence. It may also, more unpleasantly, have involved evicting villagers who may have had their huts within the defensive *burh* where Osbern planned to place his castle.

Just as history has told us virtually nothing about the location of Osbern's castle, so there has also been a deafening silence over the past use of the site in Burghill that he is likely to have chosen, though it may be significant that Burghill was later held by Harold Godwinson, perhaps again for border defence. There are no records of any other use of the site as a castle, though clearly it has been. To nineteenth-century classifiers of earthworks in Herefordshire, the site looked like a homestead moat, or defended farmhouse site, of which there were four others within three miles, but the Victoria County History of Herefordshire took note of the site and remarked: 'standing as it does in the open field and close to the church it has the appearance of having been of greater importance'. The site had been surveyed in the nineteenth century and the plan was reproduced in the County History,[18] but the volume included a note that on resurvey for the 1908 publication the site was found to have been levelled and filled. The earthwork surveyed was said to have been about 18m square with a simple

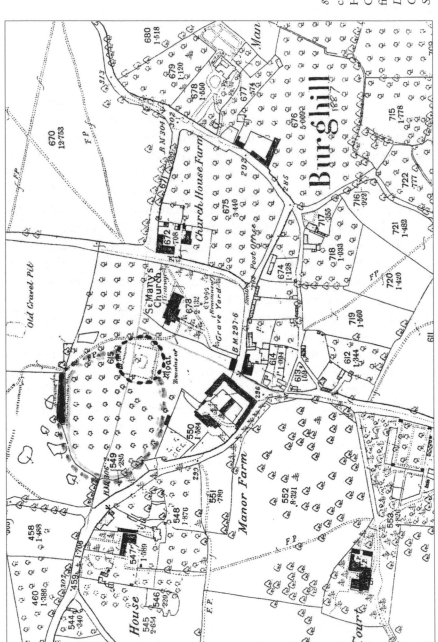

earth bank created by spoil from a surrounding moat and outside ramparts on the south and east acting as a dam to form a water level in the moat. It did not mention however that there were, and indeed still are, remains on the site of a motte and bailey castle, the most common type of castle built by the Normans, and clearly J.H. Round, in common with other historians, was not aware of the existence of a former motte and bailey castle site in one of Osbern's manors.

A Thomas Blount manuscript of about 1655[19] referred to a mound to the west of the church and a 'rampart and fosse' round what is now an orchard but would formerly have been the bailey. The motte was clearly identified on a large-scale Ordnance Survey map of 1887, and a small section of ditch and bank is still to be seen today to the north of where the motte would have been, in a situation which suggests it can only have been part of the defences of the bailey. The site is much overgrown making measurement difficult, but the top of the bank must be at least three metres above the base of the ditch if not more, and the ditch is still wet. Despite the existence of this evidence, the significance of the site was not recognised until respected Herefordshire researcher Bruce Coplestone-Crow surveyed the site in 1979. Mr Coplestone-Crow, who kindly made available his unpublished research on the site during the preparation of this book, had not regarded the site as Osbern's castle, but noted: 'A pre-Conquest castle sited at Burghill would make sense, as it dominated the Roman and post-Roman roads of Herefordshire in a way that a castle at Hereford could not'. He has also pointed out an unusual arrangement in the hundred in which Burghill was located, which supports his belief that it was the site of a pre-Conquest castle. The hundred was an administrative sub-division of the shire which, at least notionally, contained 100 hides, and other than where the hundred was spread more widely to link ecclesiastical estates, they usually covered the manors in a specific geographical area. Herefordshire's Cutsthorn Hundred however contained all the known Herefordshire pre-Conquest castles, giving the impression that someone had set up a 'rapid reaction' force in that hundred to support any castle which might come under attack. The theory is discussed more fully in Appendix B.

A further fascinating detail was added to the record of Osbern's castle by William of Malmesbury, who said that the 'invaders' had 'fortified a town in the county of Hereford'; a reference which is found nowhere else.[20] Like the chronicler, William does not give us geography more precise than the county, but his use of the word '*oppidum*', for a fortified settlement, rather than the '*castel*' used by the chronicler, suggested that he had another source not available to us. It would be possible to suggest that William had carelessly interpreted John of Worcester's use of the Latin term '*castellum*', a village or town,[21] in his reference to the fortified town, but had he done so he would surely also have followed John's misplacing of the castle in Kent. These terms could be used interchangeably by European chroniclers to refer to a fortified camp or town,[22] but these differences clearly suggest that William was using a source other than John's *Chronicle* or the *Chronicle* sources which we have today. William's reference, taken together with the annal of the chronicler, clearly suggests that Osbern had built a castle based on a fortified settlement, which is exactly what he would have been doing at Burghill.

The site would be purely defensive, but Professor Barlow has noted: 'It is impossible to believe that castles were built in the Welsh Marches for any but the obvious purpose of defending the frontier'.[23] Leading Norman castles expert Dr Derek Renn has agreed[24] that the site is likely to be pre-Conquest and one of the possible sites of Osbern's castle. Nevertheless the site has never been investigated by archaeologists, and has perhaps now been damaged so much that it might reveal little. In any event, archaeologists would not at present be able to uncover the secrets of Osbern's castle, since current methods of archaeological investigation and dating cannot distinguish between the site of a castle built 15 years before the Conquest and one built 15 years, or even 50 years, after it. So as with the reason for Osbern's occupation of the manors of Burghill and Brinsop out of all the manors in Herefordshire that he might have occupied, we can only find proof of the location of Osbern's castle by applying common sense to the interpretation of the documentary record. Given that the documentary record has shown Osbern in the two manors at the main river crossing from Wales, it is logical that the castle he built would have been nearby, and the site at Burghill was the only adjacent site which could offer him the defensive position he would need, along with a local population which could be pressed into service to refortify it. So it was undoubtedly at Burghill in Herefordshire that Osbern, the ambitious young Norman from the Cherbourg peninsula, built the first castle in England. And the evidence clearly shows that the site had a motte and bailey castle. But is that what Osbern built?

Castel, the term used to describe Osbern's castle in the *Chronicle*, was a term which invariably implied an enclosure,[25] but was the chronicler's use of the term significant? What we know without doubt is that the term was used by an Anglo-Saxon but that the word was not Anglo-Saxon. It was a foreign term, used presumably because this was a foreign construction. The use of the word makes no sense if whatever Osbern had constructed was identical to Anglo-Saxon constructions elsewhere. The chronicler was unlikely to have seen the '*castel*' at the time he wrote this entry, but those who had clearly felt it was a foreign, alien construction. So what does that tell us about the construction of the castle? It seems there was nothing unique about the elements of the Norman castle. Ditch and bank earthworks, surmounted by a defensive wall, were common in England before the Conquest, and towers were not unknown. It was the combination of these elements which was likely to have been so unfamiliar in pre-Conquest England.

However, before we can begin to solve the riddle of what Osbern's castle was like we really need to ask another, even more basic question: what was a castle? When we refer to castles we tend to think of the stone fortresses we are familiar with at Caernavon, Rochester, Alnwick and elsewhere around Britain, but the name 'castle' is often loosely applied to fortifications from earlier periods of British history. Probably the most famous of these sites is Cadbury Castle in Somerset. The hill fort at South Cadbury is believed to have been occupied from about 3000 BC until the early eleventh century and was variously a military stronghold, a centre of trade and culture and probably the focus of a religious cult – but it was never a castle as we know it. The site had earthworks which were added to over the centuries, and excavations have revealed that there were timber buildings, but nothing like the curtain fortifications of later castles. The name seems to have derived from the identification of the site as Arthur's Camelot, his base and fortress, by John Leland in 1542. Castle Dore in Cornwall was also a hill fort, dating from the Iron Age, but again the defences were earthworks. The first known reference to it was by William of Worcester in the fifteenth century, who called it 'a dilapidated castle', perhaps wrongly believing that it had formerly had wood or stone fortifications. There are other similar examples elsewhere, dating from early periods of British history, but if we are to regard a castle as a fortification or construction, whether of stone or, in many cases, especially in the early years after the Conquest, of timber, then these hill forts cannot be castles in any meaningful sense, even though they bear that name.

That it was a building or construction of some sort is undoubtedly one criteria for the identification a castle, but not the only one. Another criteria was proposed in 1912 by respected castle historian Ella Armitage, in the question: 'Did the Anglo-Saxons build castles?'[26] It had been suggested in the nineteenth century that they did, but Mrs Armitage was satisfied that was a misinterpretation of what were actually later Norman sites, and her answer was: 'As far as we know, they did not'. She had identified that an important criteria for identification of a castle was not what it was constructed from, but what use would be made of it. She insisted that the English castle only appeared 'after the establishment of the feudal system,'[27] the system of military land tenure which was brought here by the Normans. The argument seems fairly simple. The Anglo-Saxons, and the Celts before them, built fortifications for communal defence in time of war or conflict. The Norman lords built castles after 1066 for their personal defence and to emphasise their power over the Anglo-Saxons. There were inevitable differences in the construction of an Anglo-Saxon *burh*, or fortified town, and an early Norman castle, though both might use timber stockading Use was the decisive factor: it was public defence before 1066, private defence afterwards. These castles were quite different drom either Anglo-Saxon private fortified residences or burhs since though private, they had a public purpose which was aggressive rather than defensive.

In fact this simplification of Mrs Armitage's work does not sufficiently reflect the complexity of her views on the continually evolving nature of Norman castle building, but it does accurately portray her argument on supposed Anglo-Saxon castles. The subject has again been raised recently by archaeological evidence of defended private residences in Anglo-Saxon England,[28] but the excavation evidence is limited, and at the present time Mrs Armitage's argument still stands. It does however have its drawbacks. Anglo-Saxons who saw early Norman defensive constructions seem to have identified them immediately as being 'castles' – something quite different from anything which had previously existed in England, and it is questionable whether they would have done so purely on the basis of use, since there is evidence of Anglo-Saxon magnates building fortified private residences. The identification of whatever Osbern had built as a *castel* clearly implied that it appeared different to anything seen before in England, but to determine what that was we need to look at the development of castles across the Channel.

Europe also suffered Viking raids and many towns were fortified, especially under Charlemagne, but the gradual disintegration of the Carolingian empire and the rise of the feudal system, under which local magnates held land in return for military service, led to the appearance of private castles by the tenth century, though the variety of Latin terms used by contemporary writers to describe these constructions makes it difficult to determine exactly when they first appeared, or what form they took.[29] The aggressive expansion of Normandy encouraged Fulk Nerra, count of Anjou from 987 to 1044, to become an energetic castle builder,[30] a practice continued by his successor, Geoffrey Martel. Many of these early castles were probably nothing more than a ditch and bank surmounted by a wooden stockade,[31] which was not dissimilar from what might be found at Anglo-Saxon fortified *burh*s, and despite the argument put forward by Mrs Armitage, the switch from communal to private defence was probably a gradual process.

Defensive towers, mostly of wood, were known from at least 924, when one built by Herbert, count of Vermandois, burnt down. Fulk Nerra was credited with combining the two concepts to create the first motte and bailey type of castle at St Florent le Vieil on the Loire about 1010, and many of his other castles were of that type.[32] The motte, a mound possibly surrounded by a moat or ditch, with a tower on top, not only provided a final redoubt for defenders, but offered an inner sanctum as security for magnates employing mercenary soldiers whose loyalty might be questionable, and who would thus be kept at a distance in the larger fortified bailey surrounding the motte. Private castles were increasingly built without any approval from central authority, as local magnates vied with each other for power and land, and by the end of the tenth century they had become fairly common. After William of Normandy's rule was confirmed by his triumph at the battle of Val es Dunes in 1047, one of his first acts was to order the demolition of all unlicensed castles in the duchy, and the Customs of the duchy of Normandy in 1061 forbade the construction of any new unlicensed castles or defences.[33] Before 1066 there were more than 50 castles in northern France and 15 years before that date, with Osbern's arrival in Herefordshire, the castle had made its way to England.

Osbern would obviously have been familiar with the castles in his homeland, many of which would have been of motte and bailey type and of timber construction, and we might argue that his castle must have been of that type because the Anglo-Saxons thought of it as something distinctly foreign. Unfortunately things may not have been quite that simple. The word 'castel' seems to have entered common Anglo-Saxon usage by that date,[34] which suggests, but does not prove, that Anglo-Saxons were familiar with the concept of the castle as something common in Europe. Essentially, as was suggested earlier, Osbern's castle must have been reported as a 'castel' by the chronicler because Anglo-Saxons who saw it regarded it as something foreign, something not seen before in England. This may have meant that its construction was of a type not seen before in England, or that whatever its construction, they may have regarded it as a 'castel' simply because it was being built by a Norman. We can speculate on this, but we can never know what was in the minds of the Anglo-Saxons who saw this first castle being constructed, so again we need to consider what Osbern was likely to have built.

There should have been plenty of standing timber around eleventh-century Burghill to provide material to refortify the settlement, and Osbern would certainly have wanted to use some of it to construct timber stockading on top of the bank above the defensive ditch. A tower would also have been desirable, not just as a final stronghold, but because the Roman road leading to Hereford was some distance from the site, in the valley below, and would be difficult to see from the castle without a tower. Osbern had specific needs for defence and observation which meant that a timber motte and bailey castle is what he was most likely to have built, and that certainly would have seemed a foreign construction to Anglo-Saxons, who would never have seen such a thing before in England. Osbern probably did not intend it to be purely a private castle for the use of himself and his retainers alone, as would be the case with castles built after the Conquest, but he would have needed to clear the area of all but the defenders, which amounted to the same thing. A reconstruction of a typical Norman motte and bailey castle, based on historical and archaeological evidence, has been built at St Sylvain d'Anjou in northern France (see cover), though that is likely to be substantially different to Osbern's castle. The reconstruction has a strong paling wall around the bailey and a well-built roofed guard tower on the motte, but Osbern had little time to get his defences in place, which will doubtless have meant his castle was fairly roughly hewn. He may not have had the labour to do more than surmount the existing earthworks with timber fencing, and his tower is likely to have been functional and basic, quite possibly without luxuries such as a roof originally. Nevertheless it will have been the first motte and bailey castle that the Anglo-Saxons had seen. It is possible that the castle was not completed by the time that word of it was sent to Godwine in Gloucestershire, but there was clearly enough of its alien construction completed for its nature to be clear to those who saw it.

Osbern's construction works will have been obvious to any thegn remaining in the area, and no doubt he will have been approached and asked to give an account of his actions. At this point he must have given his name, but obviously it was not familiar to whoever questioned him, and given the language barrier it may not have come across clearly enough to be distinguishable. Word must quickly have been sent to Godwine in Gloucestershire that an unknown bunch of Normans were building a castle on their territory. Godwine and his sons may have seen this as the start of an attempt to establish Normans on their land while their attention was elsewhere. They were also, as the chronicler suggested, likely to see this as an affront to their power. The fact that Osbern had been sent to protect what were still at that time their lands may have been lost in translation.

As with so much in eleventh-century history, many details of Osbern's castle that we would love to have were never recorded, or have been lost in the intervening centuries, so we cannot prove beyond any possible doubt that Osbern built a motte and bailey castle at Burghill. Perhaps in the future, archaeologists will discover techniques which will enable them to confirm it. In the meantime however, there is a wealth of evidence of all kinds pointing to him having done just that, and to this Herefordshire village having been the site of the first castle in England.

Chapter Eight

Aftermath

The cataclysmic events of September 1051 brought about far-reaching changes in England which triggered a chain of events in the months that followed. There is no record of the date on which Ralph of Mantes became earl over Herefordshire, but he certainly did, and probably as soon as the Godwinesons were exiled. Undoubtedly he would have wanted to set about building a castle in the county town of Hereford, and he must also have granted lands in the county between Leominster and Ludlow to Richard fitz Scrob, who built Richard's Castle, to secure the defence of the north of the county so that England quickly progressed from its first castle to its first three.

Osbern remained on guard at the border, confirmed as the lord of the manors of Burghill and Brinsop, where the modern Herefordshire villages stand, and by 1052 he apparently had a second castle, probably commanded by his nephew, Hugo. We may never know where this second castle was sited, since aside from the fleeting reference by John of Worcester to 'castella' or castles in the 1052 annal, there is no record of this castle and no evidence of its location. Normally it would be inconceivable that a second castle would be sited as close to another as Brinsop was to Burghill, but given Osbern's mission to guard the border crossing into England it would make sense, since from Burghill he could guard the road into Hereford, but a second defensive point would have been needed beside the road running north from the ford, and Brinsop would be ideal for that. There were again some earthworks in place in Brinsop which could be re-fortified, since a site there has been identified as a likely former Roman camp. This and all the other sites connected to pre-Conquest castles are described in Appendix A. Normally the holder of a castle would be provided with a number of manors which would supply the garrison, and Osbern may have held other manors that we don't know of, but it is also possible that the earl supplied him with men and provisions since he was effectively fulfilling a specific military mission for Ralph rather than organising defence of a part of the county.

Osbern's castle and his small garrison were never tested, as far as we know. Luckily for him, the Welsh didn't come in 1051 while he was holding the border with a hastily erected castle and probably a very small force of Normans. The Welsh did come in the following year though, and somewhere near Leominster they largely wiped out a joint defensive force of Anglo-Saxons from the militia and Normans who were probably from Richard's Castle. Of where they crossed the river there is no record, but the fact that they were in the north of the county suggests they may have crossed the Wye somewhere further north, which could be because they avoided the main river crossing while it was defended by Osbern. Certainly Osbern's castle, and the others which sprang up in the following months, were just the first of many castles which would be built all over the country in the centuries that followed, playing their grim part in changing England irrevocably. Historians have argued – as historians do – about whether these changes might have come about even without the Norman Conquest, and there is little doubt that whatever happened, the importation of Norman defensive technology and military expertise would have been a continuing feature of life on the border, though Osbern's tenure there was not to be long.

For Edward also, it was the end of an era. He had finally won the battle of wills with Godwine, but he was not a young man and he now needed to turn his mind to his remaining years. According to one report, William of Normandy quickly arranged a visit to England after he heard of the Godwinesons' fate. There would have been only one subject on the agenda for his meeting with Edward: the succession. Doubtless William received Edward's usual 'nod and wink' with respect to the crown, but in his case the duke would prove to have the resources and will to hold England to Edward's word. In March of 1052 Edward's mother, Emma, the wife of two kings and mother of two more, including him, died and was buried at the Old Minster in Winchester with Cnut, the young Dane who was probably the love of her life. Whether Edward loved or hated her we will never know. Certainly he must have felt he had much to reproach her with, but he partly, perhaps largely, owed his crown to Harthacnut's 1041 invitation, which Emma was doubtless responsible for.

The Godwinesons were never likely to be down for long. In the summer of 1052 Harold sailed out from Ireland and his father from Bruges. They met on the south coast, easily evading a royal fleet partly commanded by Ralph of Mantes, and having gathered widespread support in Godwine's heartland of Kent and Sussex, they sailed up the Thames and gained support in the city of London. The whole thing was made to look easy, but it was actually a measure of the very substantial military and political skills the family possessed that they were able to evade all of Edward's defences and place him in a position where he had no choice but to restore the lands and titles of the family, and recall Edith from the nunnery where she had been languishing. All the family that is, except Swein. The black sheep of the family, whose debauching of the abbess of Leominster began Godwine's downfall, was never to return. He went barefoot from Flanders to Jerusalem, 'moved to penitence because … he had killed his cousin Beorn', said John of Worcester, but he fell ill and died in excessive cold as he returned.

By then England had three Norman ecclesiastics, Archbishop Robert, William Bishop of London and Ulf Bishop of Lincoln, and all three, with their Norman retainers, fled the country. William, who was said to be a good man, was shortly afterwards recalled to his see, but Robert, who had done as much as anyone to create the political crisis of 1051, never returned to England. Despite claims that there was a general exodus of Normans, there seem to have been no other major departures. Ralph remained as earl over Herefordshire and Richard fitz Scrob remained in control of defence in the north of the county. But it was obviously a point of principle with Godwine that the castle in Herefordshire, which had so angered him during the political crisis of the previous year, had to go, even though Ralph was now earl of the county, not Swein. A stronger earl might have resisted Godwine's demand, but Ralph did not. Osbern didn't flee, though he may have seen this coming and had found a new lord in the ill-fated Scottish king, Macbeth. He and Hugo made a dignified exit, surrendering their castles and passing through Mercia to Scotland with a safe conduct from Leofric. Osbern's castles were probably burnt, or torn down and the timber reused. No doubt Osbern's countrymen built a stone castle on the site at Burghill some time after the Conquest, though there is no record and nothing remains of it. Two years after Osbern's departure from Herefordshire Macbeth was defeated by Siward of Northumbria and, according to John of Worcester, all the Normans in Macbeth's service were killed. So ended the life and career of a man with a unique place in our historical record. Osbern was probably only in his mid-twenties and had had very little luck with the lords he had served, but he had built the first castle in England, and thus found a permanent place of honour in the annals of English history.

Ralph must have lived to regret letting Osbern be removed from the border. In 1055 there was no-one in place to oppose a joint force of Welshmen, Vikings and rebel Mercians crossing the border, doubtless at the ford that Osbern had defended. Ralph met them outside Hereford with a joint force of Normans and Anglo-Saxons. It was a major test of his skill in military innovation, and he failed miserably. Traditionally, mounted English militiamen rode to a battle but fought on foot; however Ralph was determined that they would fight on horseback like Normans. Chroniclers and historians disagreed over whether it was the English or the Normans who precipitated the rout, but Ralph and his whole force fled before the battle even began. The raiders pursued them towards Hereford and killed many before pillaging and burning the city. Little wonder that history remembers Edward's nephew as Ralph the Timid. The only surprise is that William of Normandy, who surely can't have met him, once regarded Ralph as a competitor for the throne of England. Ralph died in December 1057, and Harold Godwineson became earl over Herefordshire, pacifying the border and the whole of Wales over the next six years.

After the restoration of 1052, Edward and Godwine seem to have declared a draw and settled into an apparently peaceful coexistence, but it was not to last long. On Easter Monday 1053, as Godwine sat at dinner with the king at Winchester, he had a seizure. It left him speechless and in great pain, and three days later the man who had risen from obscure beginnings to create the most powerful family in Anglo-Saxon England, died. He was buried at the Old Minster in Winchester, capital of his earldom of Wessex, where his master, Cnut, lay. Harold Godwineson succeeded to his father's earldom, but he already seemed to have adopted a broader view than his father's focus on the family, and Harold's former earldom in the east went to Aelfgar, Leofric of Mercia's son. Over the next 12 years Harold seemed to take over many of the routine tasks of administration in the kingdom and when Edward died, early in 1066, it was said he named Harold his successor on his deathbed. Thus Godwine, whose burning desire to have a grandson on the throne of England was frustrated, instead had a son on the throne, but not for long: in late September 1066, fifteen years after the Godwinesons were exiled from England, William of Normandy landed his invasion fleet at Pevensey and England was changed forever.

One final mystery remains. Since the pre-Conquest castle at Ewyas Harold was not built by Osbern, who did build it? It has been suggested above that it must have been an 'official' castle built for strategic defence, probably by a substantial landowner such as the earl of Hereford. Ralph, Edward's Norman nephew and earl of Hereford probably from late 1051, might seem the obvious candidate, but Ewyas Harold was still very much in Welsh territory at Ralph's death. It is also worth noting that Ralph, whom William of Malmesbury styled 'indolent and cowardly', couldn't stop the Welsh two miles from Hereford, so the likelihood of him venturing miles into their territory and setting about castle building seems extremely remote. The only other castle-building Norman in the shire was Richard Fitz Scrob of Richard's Castle, but there is no reason to suppose that he would venture this far south and no sign in Domesday of any landholding by him in the area.

The only other possible candidate was Harold Godwineson, who was effectively the power in Herefordshire from 1055 and assumed the earldom on Ralph's death, if not before. As England's last Saxon king and the man who died fighting the Normans for control of England he might seem an odd choice as builder of a 'Norman' castle, but Harold was an innovative soldier and there is no reason to suppose that he would have shown the bloody-minded xenophobia of which he is usually accused in relation to the appearance of Norman castles in England. The man whose lightning marches, reminiscent of marines 'yomping' across the Falklands, almost startling enemies into submission is likely to have taken careful note of any new military ideas, especially when examples had appeared on his Herefordshire doorstep. Certainly after 1055 it must have been clear that some defensive position was needed to protect the crossing into England, and after Harold's incursions into Wales it could usefully be placed further west than Burghill, where it could give greater advance warning of a raid. In centuries past there was a local tradition that Harold did build the castle at Ewyas Harold and that he gave his name to the village, though it has been discounted by historians who prefer to believe that it was Ralph's son, also Harold, who gave his name to the village when he received the manor from the king around 1086. Leland, who visited the area around 1538, wrote, 'The fame is that the castle was builded of Harold afore he was king, and when he overcame the Welshmen Harold gave this castle to his bastard.'[1] Domesday showed that Harold was the holder *TRE* of a dozen manors in Straddele and Archenfield, though whether he also held Ewyas Harold is unknown.

If having defeated the Welshmen, as tradition suggested, Harold gave the castle at Ewyas Harold to his bastard, then he was somewhat spoilt for choice, having, according to the chronicle, at least three illegitimate sons, Godwine, Eadmund and Magnus, who took refuge in Ireland after the Conquest and mounted piratical raids on the West Country in 1068 and 69, but we look in vain for their names in *TRE* landholdings in Archenfield and Straddele. In any event none of this troublesome trio fit the bill for Leland's 'bastard', who was supposedly called Harold after his father, and doesn't appear in *TRE* landholdings either, and even worse, though Leland was probably referring to Ewyas Harold, his information is so confused that we can't be certain.

Perhaps the strongest evidence for Harold's construction of Ewyas Harold is that having discounted Osbern's connection, and given the castle's strategic location and nature, there is really no-one else who could be responsible for it. In detective story terms, Harold seems to be the only person who had both the motive and the opportunity to build a castle at Ewyas Harold, and if he did, then he has the distinction of being the only Anglo-Saxon to have built a 'Norman' castle in England, but since Ewyas Harold Castle seems to have been built primarily for community defence, to keep the Welsh raiders out of Herefordshire, though it may have been Norman in style it was Anglo-Saxon in spirit.

Appendix A

Pre-Conquest Castles

It is not possible to determine by means of archaeological evidence whether a castle is pre- or post-Conquest, so the evidence for the pre-Conquest existence of these sites rests on documentary sources which can be fairly sparse and often are not completely clear, but they are sufficient, taken together with other available information about the sites and their builders, to prove the likely pre-Conquest existence of the sites listed below.

Burghill, near Hereford

The former existence of a motte and bailey castle on a site to the west of the parish church in Burghill was first spotted by respected Herefordshire researcher Bruce Coplestone-Crow in 1979. He kindly supplied the site information below while this book was in preparation.

A motte and bailey castle, that may well be pre-Conquest in date, formerly stood to the west of the church; traces of the bailey can still be seen. Thomas Blount, writing c.1655, said a mound stood to the west of the church and that a 'rampart and fosse' surrounded the then existing orchard (the relevant quotation from his MS hangs in the parish church). The ditch on the north was still partly wet when inspected. There are now houses in the bailey and their driveways to them cross the site of the ditch and bank.

When the motte and bailey was built the roads near the church were diverted. The motte and most of the bailey were levelled at some point, probably when Manor Farm was enlarged at the end of the seventeenth century. The square feature that replaced the motte was probably an ornamental fish pond within the farm's garden.

The motte and bailey would seem to have covered about 1.5ha (quite large) and could well have been pre-Conquest in origin. A pre-Conquest castle sited at Burghill would make sense as it dominated the Roman and post-Roman roads of Herefordshire in a way that a castle at Hereford could not.

Brinsop, near Hereford

The existence of a second castle, probably held by Osbern's nephew, Hugo, in 1052, is all the evidence we have here, so exact identification of a site is not possible, but as we know that Osbern held this manor, about five miles beyond Hereford and near Burghill, a castle there would make sense in terms of defence of the border crossing, and there was apparently a former defensive site there which could have been re-fortified. Earthworks beside the parish church there have been attributed to Roman times.[1] Some doubts were expressed by the Victoria County History of Hereford about the site's Roman origins, but the manor was close to the Roman town of Magna,[2] and a well from the period was discovered in Brinsop in 1887,[3] so clearly there was Romano-British occupation in the area. The rectangular site, shown by the County History plan to be about 25m wide and just over double that in length, is beside a stream and the site survey[4] showed the watercourse and a marsh protected it on the south and east, with earth banks and ditches which were thought to have formed a moat. Sadly since that survey much of the site has been levelled and the more recent creation of a series of lakes, probably for land drainage and flood relief, has obscured the line of the stream.

This site would have been very much the right size for a force of up to 20 mounted men with room for picketing of horses, storage of supplies and cooking fires. There is no evidence that a motte ever stood on the site but castle historians have been emphasising at least since Mrs Armitage in 1912 that not all Norman castles were necessarily of the motte and bailey type; she pointed to the probability that 'the earliest castles built in Normandy were without mottes and were simple enclosures'.[5] This is very likely to have been true of the site at Brinsop, which already had good natural protection on two sides and would probably have needed only the addition of a timber paling wall to make it sufficient for Osbern's purposes and equal to many early castles in Normandy, some of which might have been still extant in that form. The site at Brinsop does not have the commanding position or the potential strategic significance of Burghill and if it was indeed the site of Osbern's second castle, or rather Hugo's castle, it represents a quite different order of development, being a local base rather than a strategic fortification. No doubt there was later manorial use of the site and that seems to be how it is regarded by historians today. The site has not been excavated.

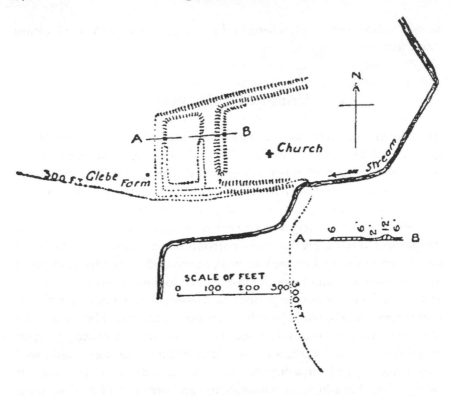

9 The former Roman camp at Brinsop which may have been utilised by Osbern as his second castle.

Hereford

There was only one pre-Conquest reference to a castle in Hereford, when it was said to have been destroyed by the Welsh in 1055.[6] It seems likely that Ralph of Mantes, having been appointed to the earldom, probably in late 1051, would have wanted a castle in Hereford. The Historic Towns publication covering Hereford suggests speculatively, without supporting evidence or argument, that Ralph probably built Hereford Castle 'before 1052' and subsequently that the king 'often' stayed in the city 'probably in the castle', but was unable to identify a site, though it did map a suggested royal palace in the bailey of the later Norman castle near where St Guthlac's monastery was sited until the twelfth century.[7] 'Palace' may be something of a misnomer in this instance since the building may have been more in the nature of a hunting lodge. Edward's love of hunting was well known, and after holding court at Gloucester, as he regularly did, his visits to Hereford were more likely to have been for pleasure than business. Domesday showed that the burgesses of Hereford had a duty to act as beaters for him, and the men of the village of Kingstone were required to drag back to the city whatever he happened to have shot.

It was the former city archaeologist, Ron Shoesmith, who suggested that a pre-Conquest castle might have stood on Hogg's Mount, a towering hill bordering the bailey of the later castle. The bailey is now a park known as Castle Green. The Hogg's Mount site has not been excavated, and any pre-Conquest archaeological remains that there might have been were probably badly damaged by the construction of the later curtain walls of a substantial stone castle, their demolition, or the site's conversion into pleasure gardens after the civil war. It is not possible to describe what this castle may have been like, since no remains exist, but if the castle was on Hogg's Mount it was occupying the same sort of towering strategic defensive site as Richard's Castle, which is the sort of site the earl might be expected to choose for his castle.

Richard's Castle, north Herefordshire

A single vague chronicle reference supports the existence of Richard's Castle, between Leominster in Herefordshire and Ludlow in Shropshire, but as with Clavering there is important post-Conquest evidence. Richard fitz Scrob's arrival in Herefordshire, probably in 1052,[8] presumably in response to the exile of Godwine and his sons, and perhaps at the request or suggestion of either Edward or his nephew Ralph, and his son Osbern's holding of a wooden castle, Castle Avreton, at Domesday, do tend to suggest an early castle and this seems to be confirmed by a 1067 *Chronicle* reference to the castlemen of Hereford and Richard's men in action against Edric the Wild, though there is no mention of Richard's Castle. The castle seems clearly intended for strategic defence, situated on high ground commanding wide views over the north Herefordshire border area and the route into the county from the north.

The remains, of both earthworks and some standing masonry, show that the castle possessed a motte and kidney-shaped bailey both ditched, with the circular motte standing some 60ft above the ditch, and outer works which show that a ditch and bank also once enclosed the nearby church and perhaps the original village,[9] although the village has now, not surprisingly, moved down the hill. The site is impressive and clearly would only have been chosen by someone who had some motivation for not just personal defence but defence of the area and perhaps the county, and someone who had the time to develop the site. The towering motte may not have existed before the Conquest but the steep hill leading to the site certainly did. This site has the look of one chosen by someone with an established position in the area and every reason to expect a long-term future there, all of which seems to have been true of Richard fitz Scrob. The site has been excavated by archaeologists in recent times, but not surprisingly no evidence of a

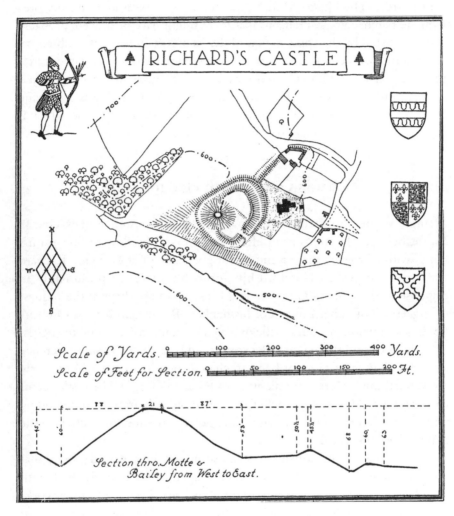

10 Site plan of the medieval motte and bailey castle which replaced a pre-Conquest timber castle built by Richard fitz Scrob in 1052.

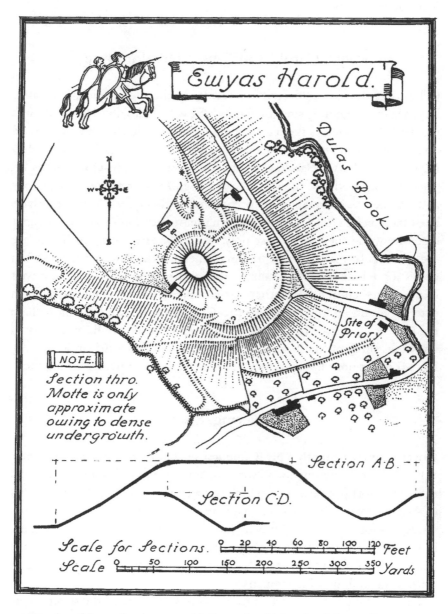

11 Site plan of the medieval motte and bailey castle which replaced the pre-Conquest castle on the site.

pre-Conquest castle was found, the later stone castle having no doubt obliterated any traces.

Ewyas Harold, south-west Herefordshire

Osbern's castle was mislocated by Freeman at the site of Richard's Castle, but equally erroneously sited by Round at Ewyas Harold in Herefordshire's Golden Valley. Round's theory, accepted for more than a century, was based on information in Domesday. The survey proved that the castle refortified by fitz Osbern at Ewyas Harold after the Conquest was a pre-Conquest castle, since it is believed that fitz Osbern arrived in Herefordshire early in 1067 and returned to Normandy in 1070, so any castle he refortified must have been there before 1066. Of fitz Osbern's refortification or any subsequent defensive works there is no trace now, except for earthworks, including the site of a circular motte almost 70m in diameter at the base, towering 50ft in places above kidney-shaped bailey earthworks on a spur about 300yds west of the village church.[10] Whether this commanding site, over two acres in extent,[11] is entirely the work of a pre-Conquest castle builder or William fitz Osbern or one of his successors at Ewyas Harold we have no way of knowing. Alfred of Marlborough was the holder of Ewyas Harold in 1086. Recent excavations have produced evidence of later buildings on the site.

Clavering, Essex

Clavering was apparently a pre-Conquest site but it was not a castle as such. It was built by a Breton, not a Norman, but more significantly it was not a castle but a fortified residence, which was a type of building already familiar to Anglo-Saxons since native magnates had constructed such fortified residences for themselves.[12] It is included here to avoid confusion, because it was referred to as a castle in a pre-Conquest source, probably because the chronicler, who doubtless hadn't seen it, assumed that it must be a castle since it was built by a Frenchman.

The case for pre-Conquest existence of this site rests on the single vague 1052 chronicle entry, which confirmed the existence of a castle owned by Robert, presumably somewhere north of London, when the Godwinesons returned in 1052. The possible candidates for ownership of this castle were Robert of Jumieges, archbishop from 1051, and Robert the son of a Breton woman named Wymarc and a staller or official under Edward, who had come to England with him or soon afterwards in Harthacnut's reign. Amazingly Freeman and Round actually agreed on the latter.

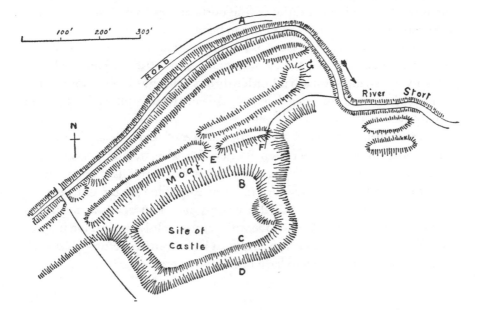

12 Plan of the site at Clavering where Robert fitz Wymarc built a fortified residence, referred to as a castle in the *Chronicle*.

To the chronicler there was probably no distinction between Norman and Breton – they were all from across the Channel – but it is questionable why the Normans would flee to the protection of someone who was not one of their own. Presumably in a crisis it was their only option, and Robert must have possessed the skill to maintain good relations with all parties at court, helped with the Normans by a common language.

It was J.H. Round who proposed Clavering as Robert fitz Wymarc's 'castle', since it was 'the greatest manor held by him in Essex',[13] as attested by Domesday, though the Victoria County History of Essex notes – not written by Round – said that the surviving earthworks could be either pre- or post-Conquest. Robert fitz Wymarc had been in the country for many years prior to 1052 and he could have built his fortified residence at Clavering at some earlier date, but Essex was held by Harold Godwineson until the exile of Godwine and his sons in 1051, and it is unlikely that the family would have welcomed such a development while they held Essex. After their exile he would have had the leisure to create his residence at Clavering. Robert's son Suen held the hundred at Domesday. There was no mention in the survey of a castle at Clavering, but the same is true of Hereford where there was clearly a castle by 1067.

The surviving earthworks show a rectangular site about 300 by 185ft and 16 or 17ft above the level of the surrounding moat which was fed by the River Stort running nearby on the north and east sides. Masonry walls were reported in 1768 'not long since in being'.[14] No excavations have been carried out on the site, and there is no information on the early use of the site, but it must have been very different to the castles in Herefordshire, which were facing substantial border threats, and thus it was more in the nature of a fortified residence than any castle in Herefordshire of that period could have been.

There is firm evidence, as mentioned above, of Robert's 'castle' in 1052 and a clear connection between Robert fitz Wymarc and Clavering, as well as obvious proof of a 'castle' there. What we do not have are the links to connect these proofs together in an unassailable case for Clavering as Robert's 'castle', but given that this was his most important manor in the county we have to take Round's identification seriously, and though it is not positively proven this seems very likely to have been Robert fitz Wymarc's 'castle' and was most likely to have been built in early 1052.

Appendix B

The Cutsthorn Hundred

It has been suggested, by respected Herefordshire researcher Mr Bruce Coplestone-Crow in a letter to the author, that the unique arrangement of Herefordshire's Cutsthorn Hundred supports the pre-Conquest existence of Herefordshire castles at Burghill, Richard's Castle, Ewyas Harold and Hereford. The relevant section of Mr Coplestone-Crow's letter reads as follows:

> One curiosity of the local administration of Herefordshire in the time of Edward the Confessor (as shown in Domesday Book) is that the possible pre-Conquest castle at Burghill, plus the ones at Richard's Castle and Ewyas Harold, all lay in the same hundred (Cutsthorn), despite their wide geographical separation. This hundred also surrounded the city of Hereford, the probable site of a fourth pre-Conquest castle, on its east and north sides. No other 1066 hundred in Herefordshire was split three ways like this. The reason for it was probably that someone, probably Ralph of Mantes, earl in the county, reorganized them with an eye to bringing the areas surrounding the major castles of the time under one administration. This was important because the fyrd or local militia was called out hundred by hundred. It could be therefore that the intention was to use the Cutsthorn fyrd for the initial defence of one or other of these castles, if threatened (there being, as yet, no feudal system to take care of such emergencies), before reinforcements could be brought up by the earl or his Norman associates. The earl's catastrophic attempt to make the English fight on horseback like Norman knights [see *Chronicle* 1055] was probably part and parcel of the same scheme.

Using the men of this hundred as a countywide quick reaction force to give rapid protection to any castle in the county until more forces could be called out, is the sort of military improvement that a European-trained knight such as Ralph might have sought to introduce in the absence of a feudal system of knight's duties. Ralph's military skills were not much admired, with good reason, but his attempt to get the Anglo-Saxons fighting on horseback, disastrous though it turned out to be when tested in battle, does show him to have been a military innovator, seeking to bring European thinking into the organization of defence in his county of Herefordshire while he was earl. Whether he introduced such schemes into other earldoms he is believed to have held, as discussed previously, is unknown, but there was a particular need for well-organized defence in Herefordshire because of the threat from Wales, which did not exist in the East Midlands or in Worcestershire and Warwickshire, where he is also believed to have held power.

The concept is not entirely proven, since there is no certainty when or by whom the arrangement of this hundred was first made. The only source we have is Domesday Book, and post-Conquest changes or additions had clearly been made to the hundred by 1086. For example, of the two references to Ewyas Harold in this hundred, one relates to land in the castlery given by William Fitz Osbern, post-Conquest earl of Hereford, which suggests the holding had been placed in the Cutsthorn hundred post-conquest, and the second appears to relate to the king's three churches in Archenfield, referred to in Domesday Book, and could be either pre- or post-Conquest.

The vast majority of the manors or landholdings included in the hundred are clustered around Hereford itself, which may well suggest that Ralph was putting in place the forces he needed to protect a castle at Hereford, but does not in itself support the idea of a force to protect whatever other castles existed, since no manors near either Richards Castle or Ewyas Harold are included. Castles at Burghill and Hereford were not included in the hundred at Domesday, but then neither were Ewyas Harold and Richard's Castle, for which there is also pre-Conquest evidence. A table showing the parishes included in the hundred is shown opposite, with manors containing projected pre-Conquest castles in bold type.

Harold Godwinson could have created this hundredal arrangement after he became earl over Herefordshire, but Ralph of Mantes seems the most likely candidate, and though the evidence does not permit any definite conclusions, the unusual form of this hundred, and the fact that all likely pre-Conquest castle sites are included in it strongly supports Mr Coplestone-Crow's theory.

Manor	Ref.	Holder	Notes
Hampton Bishop	182b	The Canons of Hereford	
Tupsley	182b	The Canons of Hereford	
Shelwick	182b	The Canons of Hereford	Two holdings.
Sugwas	182b	The Canons of Hereford	
Warham	182b	The Canons of Hereford	
Canon Pyon	182b	The Canons of Hereford	
Huntingdon	182b	The Canons of Hereford	
Holmer	182b	The Canons of Hereford	
Moreton on Lugg	182b	The Canons of Hereford	
Pipe	182c	The Canons of Hereford	
Lyde	182c	The Canons of Hereford	
Credenhill	182c	The Canons of Hereford	
Ewyas Harold	184a	Roger de Lacy	'In the castlery of Ewias Earl William gave [land] to Walter de Lacy.' So this holding arose only after the conquest, when the castle was being refortified, and was then added to the hundred. Ewyas Harold castle is not assigned to any hundred.
Stretton (Sugwas)	184b	Roger de Lacy	
Lyde	184b	Roger de Lacy	
Lyde	184b	Roger de Lacy	
Richards Castle	185b	Robert Gernon	Land in the castlery.
Ewyas Harold	185b	Henry de Ferrers	Three churches with 32 acres [prob. burial land] in the castlery. Two dwellings in the castle [prob. clerics' accomm.]. These are presumably the king's three churches in Archenfield (ref 179b) and were probably added to the hundred by William Fitz Osbern.
Burghill	186a	Alfred of Marlborough	
Brinsop	186a	Alfred of Marlborough	
Litley	186c	Durand of Gloucester	
Lyde	186d	Osbern Fitz Richard	Osbern's castle at Richards Castle is not assigned to any hundred.
Wellington	187b	Hugh Lasne	Two holdings.
Credenhill	187b	Hugh Lasne	
Stretton (Sugwas)	187b	Hugh Lasne	

Notes

Chapter One – Dawn of a Troubled Century

1 Stafford, p.211
2 Crouch, pp26–7
3 p.24
4 ii p.7
5 *op. cit.* pp5–7
6 *op. cit.* p.7
7 Brown, p.21
8 Freeman, i p.167
9 Stenton, p.373
10 p.374
11 Crossley-Holland, intro
12 pp54–8
13 Enc. p.93
14 pp16–17
15 *op. cit.*
16 2004 p.11
17 O'Brien, p.15
18 p.380
19 Colvin, i p.10
20 Barlow, 1970 p.10
21 ii p.44–7
22 Stenton, p.384
23 *ibid.*
24 Lawson, 2004 p.223
25 p.394

Chapter Two – England Conquered

1 p.150
2 p.31
3 Stenton, p.399
4 Introduction
5 p.31
6 Lawson, p.135
7 *Encomium* Ap. III p.70
8 p.33
9 *ibid.*
10 Linklater, p.133
11 p.398
12 O'Brien, p.101
13 cxxvi
14 p.33
15 *ibid.*
16 xxi
17 p.35
18 ii pp244–5
19 p.37
20 Lawson, p.122
21 Crossley-Holland, p.28
22 p.411
23 p.9
24 *Vita*, p.10 n.16
25 Mason, p.33
26 Barlow, 2002 p.18

Chapter Three – The Rise of Godwine

1 Stenton, pp403-4
2 p.405
3 Barlow, 2002 p.20
4 *ibid.*
5 Lavelle, app. 2
6 p.31
7 pp10-11
8 Barlow, *op. cit.* p.23
9 Enc. p.282
10 i p.314
11 p.417
12 i p.192
13 Williams, p.330
14 p.11
15 pp10-11
16 Stenton, p.398
17 p.39
18 p.35
19 Barlow, *op. cit.* p.29
20 Campbell, p.208
21 pp40-41
22 *ibid.*
23 pp32-3
24 *Encomium* xxxii
25 pp40-41
26 xxxiii
27 p.240
28 pp42-5, xxxi
29 pp32-3
30 ii pp176-7
31 p.421
32 pp52-3
33 Enc. p.229
34 pp52-3
35 Williams, p.335

Chapter Four – Seeds of Quarrel

1 Barlow, 1970 p.13
2 pp34-5
3 Barlow, *op. cit.* p.29 & n.4
4 *op. cit.* p.38
5 *op. cit.* p.39
6 *op. cit.* p.40
7 xxx
8 Barlow, *op. cit.* p.58
9 pp14-15
10 *ibid.*
11 p.17
12 Williams, p.327
13 Barlow, *op. cit.* pp51-2
14 *Vita* lxiv
15 Lawson, 2004 p.172
16 Barlow, 1988 p.55
17 Mason, p.35
18 Barlow, 2002 p.33
19 *Vita* pp22-3
20 *ibid.*
21 pp259-60
22 xxxix
23 pp14-5
24 p.92
25 lxxvii
26 Stafford, p.261
27 Barlow, 1970 p.93
28 Barlow, *op. cit.* pp25, 93
29 p.425
30 p.424
31 pp48-51, 80
32 pp18-9
33 Barlow, *op. cit.* p.95

Chapter Five – The Final Act

1 Turvey, pp19–29
2 Mason, p.54
3 *ibid.*
4 Heming, Cartulary, ed Hearne 275-6, quoted in VCHW ii 5
5 Barlow, 1970 pp102–3
6 pp28–9
7 *Vita* pp30–1
8 Barlow, *op. cit.* p.105
9 pp30–33
10 *Vita* pp32–5
11 Barlow, 2002 p.44
12 Stenton, p.429
13 Barlow, 1970 p.104
14 Williams, p.327
15 Barlow, *op. cit.* p.93
16 pp60–1
17 Barlow, 1970 p.109
18 pp307–8
19 *op. cit.*
20 p.39
21 Barlow, 2002 p.43
22 Barlow, 1970 p.109
23 Walker, p.181
24 pp32–5

Chapter Six – The Hunt for Osbern's Castle

1 p.562 n.1
2 VCHE i pp291–3
3 p.563
4 VCHH p.353
5 p.283
6 Round ppxii, 332–3
7 Ekwall, p.412: but see Lawson, 2002 pp57–9
8 Powell p.95
9 Barlow, 2002 p.5
10 Stephens, Preface
11 *The Athenaeum* No. 3526, 25 May 1895, p.675
12 Powell pp104–5
13 *The History and Antiquities of Colchester Castle*, Benham & Co, Colchester, see Powell, Bibliography of the publications of J.H. Round
14 Powell p.96
15 *op. cit.* pp98–100
16 pp334–8
17 p.320
18 p.333
19 xiii
20 p.718
21 Powell p.94
22 ii p561–2
23 Williams p.329
24 ii p.138
25 p.351
26 pp329–331
27 p.325
28 p.562
29 pp99–100
30 p.39
31 p.8
32 ii p.138
33 ii p.138, 331, also v. p.649
34 pp322–4
35 pp352–3
36 VCHE p.345
37 pp351–2
38 p.85
39 p.562
40 iii p.xlix
41 p.5
42 p.100–1, *English Castles* p.22
43 p.562 n1
44 p.324

45 p.352
46 1986 pp384-5
47 Marshall, p.141
48 *op. cit.* p.142
49 Keynes, p.71
50 Enc. p.341
51 Coplestone-Crow, Sep 1992, p.9
52 DB H Note 1

53 VCHH p.266
54 Turvey, p.25
55 *ibid.*
56 VCHH p.264
57 Darby, pp109-110
58 *op. cit.*
59 1989 p.109; Jan 1992 p.7
60 Darby, p.53

Chapter Seven – The First Castle

1 Coplestone-Crow, 1986 p.376
2 Round, pp327-8
3 Coplestone-Crow, *op. cit.* p.377
4 Op. cit. p.378
5 Op. cit. p,376
6 Glover
7 p.285
8 1985 p.38
9 Orderic Vitalis ii xxx
10 Gravett, p.72
11 Orderic Vitalis xxxvi
12 SMR Herefordshire
13 RCHM Herefordshire iii pl
14 Hale, p.327
15 Op. cit. pp331-2
16 Blake
17 Ekwall, p.75

18 p.249
19 Harleien manuscripts, British Library, also displayed in Burghill Church
20 OUP i pp358-9
21 Armitage pp383-4
22 *op. cit.* pp68, 384
23 1970 p.94
24 Letter to the author
25 Armitage p.384
26 p.11
27 viii
28 Higham, p.39
29 Armitage, pp66, 68
30 *op. cit.* pp72-3
31 *op. cit.* p.71
32 *op. cit.* p.73
33 Renn, p.4

Chapter Eight – Aftermath

1 v 177

Appendix A

1 VCHH p.252
2 *op. cit.* p.175
3 *op. cit.* p.191
4 *op. cit.* p.252
5 p.78 n.1
6 Jones p.25
7 Lobel Hfd p.2

8 Stenton, p.352
9 RCHM Herefordshire ii p.172
10 *op. cit.* i pp63-4
11 Armitage, sched.
12 Higham, p.39
13 VCHE p.345
14 Op. cit. p.292

Bibliography and
Abbreviations

Allen-Brown, R.

—— *The Normans and the Norman Conquest*, 2nd edn. (Boydell Press 1985)

—— *English Castles*, (Batsford 1962, 3rd edn. 1976)

—— 1970 'An Historian's Approach to the Origins of the Castle in England', *The Archaeological Journal* vol. CXXVI

Armitage, E.S., *The Early Norman Castles of the British Isles* (John Murray 1912)

Bannister, A.T.

—— *The History of Ewias Harold: its Castle, Priory and Church*, (Jakeman & Carver, Hereford, 1902)

—— 1904 'The Herefordshire Domesday', *TWC*

Barlow, F.

—— *Edward the Confessor* (University of California Press 1970)

—— *The Feudal Kingdom of England 1042-1216*, 4th edn. (Longman 1988)

—— *The Godwins: The Rise and Fall of a Noble Dynasty* (Longman 2002)

Bede, *A History of the English Church and People*, trans. Sherley-Price, L., rev. (Penguin 1968)

Blake, W.A., *Parish of Burghill, Herefordshire* (1972, no publisher)

Boucher, A., *Ewyas Harold Castle* (Archaeological Investigations Ltd., undated)

Campbell, J., ed., *The Anglo-Saxons* (Penguin 1991)

Chronicle: *The Anglo-Saxon Chronicle(s)*. Editions used:

—— *The Anglo-Saxon Chronicle*, trans Garmonsway, G.N., 2nd edn (Dent 1954)

—— *The Anglo-Saxon Chronicle*, trans Whitelock, D., with Douglas, D.C. and Tucker, S.I. (Eyre and Spottiswood 1961)

—— *The Anglo-Saxon Chronicles*, Swanton, M., rev edn (Phoenix Press 2000)

Colvin, H.M., ed., *The History of the King's Works* (HMSO 1963)

Coplestone-Crow, B.

—— 1986 'The Fief of Alfred of Marlborough in Herefordshire in 1086 and its Descent in the Norman Period', *TWC* 1986

—— 1989 'Herefordshire Place-Names', BAR British Series 214

—— 1992 'The Castle of Ewyas Harold and its Military Arrangements in the Norman Period', *HAN* 57 Jan 1992

—— 1992 'Welsh Kings and their Lands in Herefordshire', *HAN* 58 Sep. 1992

—— 1993 'Medieval Topography of Ewyas Harold', *HAN* 60 Sep. 1993

Crossley-Holland, K., ed. & trans., *The Anglo-Saxon World*, new edn. (Boydell Press 2002)

Crouch, D., *The Normans: The History of a Dynasty* (Hambledon & London 2002)

Darby, H.C. & Terrett, I.B., eds. *The Domesday Geography of Midland England* (CUP 1954)

Domesday Book:

—— (Penguin 2002)

—— Herefordshire, eds. Thorn, F. & C, (Phillimore 1983)

Ekwall, E., *The Concise Oxford Dictionary of English Place-Names*, 4th edn. (OUP 1960)

Enc.: *The Blackwell Encyclopaedia of Anglo-Saxon England*, ed. Lapidge, M. *et al.* (Blackwell 2001)

Encomium: *Encomium Emmae Reginae*, ed. Campbell, A., supp. int. Keynes, S., new edn. (CUP 1998)

Finberg, H.P.R., *The Early Charters of the West Midlands* (Leicester University Press 1961)

Florence of Worcester: *A History of the Kings of England*, ed. & trans. Stevenson, J., Seeleys London 1853 (reprint Llanerch Press 1996)

Fox, C., *Offa's Dyke: A Field Survey of the Western Frontier Works of Mercia in the Seventh and Eighth Centuries AD* (OUP 1955)

Freeman, E.A., *The History of the Norman Conquest: Its Causes and its Results*, 6 vols (Oxford 1867–1873)

Glover, R., *Visitation of Cheshire 1580*, ed. Rylands, J.P. (London 1882)

Gravett, C. & Nicolle, D., *The Normans: Warrior Knights and their Castles* (Osprey 2007)

Hale, M., 1968 'Roman Roads in Herefordshire', *TWC* XXXIX

HAN – Herefordshire Archaeological News

Henry of Huntingdon:

—— *The History of the English People 1000-1154*, trans. Greenway, D., (OUP 2002)

—— *The Chronicle of Henry of Huntingdon*, ed. & trans. Forester, T., Seeleys London 1853 (reprint Llanerch Press, 1991)

Higham, R. & Barker, P., *Timber Castles* (University of Exeter Press 2004)

Howorth, H., 1916 'The Chronicle of John of Worcester previously assigned to Florence of Worcester', The Archaeological Journal vol. LXXIII 1-4

HSMR: 'Roman Roads in Herefordshire', www.smr.herefordshire.gov.uk

Jackson, J.N., 1954 'The Historical Geography of Herefordshire, from Saxon Times to the Act of Union, 1536', *TWC* ch. XIII

John of Fordun: *Chronicle of the Scottish Nation*, Edinburgh 1872 (reprint Llanerch Press 1993)

John of Worcester: *The Chronicle of John of Worcester*, eds. Darlington, R.R. and McGurk, P.; trans. Bray, J. and McGurk, P., vol. II (OUP 1995)

Jones, T., ed. & trans., *Brut y Tywysogyon* – The Chronicle of the Princes, Red Book of Hergest version (Cardiff 1955)

Keynes, S. and Lapidge, M., trans., *Alfred the Great* (Penguin 1983)

Lavelle, R., *Aethelred II: King of the English 978-1016* (Tempus 2002)

Lawson, M.K.:

—— *Cnut: England's Viking King* (Tempus 2004)

—— *The Battle of Hastings 1066* (Tempus 2002)

Leland: *Itinerary*, (5 vols) ed. Smith, L.T. (Centaur 1964)

Linklater, E., *The Conquest of England* (Hodder & Stoughton 1966)

Lobel, M.D., *Historic Towns*, vol. I (Lovell Johns 1969)

Marshall, G., 1938 'The Norman Occupation of the Lands in the Golden Valley, Ewyas and Clifford and their Motte and Bailey Castles', *TWC* 1936-8

Mason, E., *The House of Godwine: The History of a Dynasty* (Hambledon and London 2004)

Myres, A., *The English Settlements* (OUP)

O'Brien, H., *Queen Emma and the Vikings* (Bloomsbury 2005)

Orderic Vitalis: *The Ecclesiastical History*, ed. & trans. Chibnall, M., 6 vols. 1969–1980, vol II paperback (OUP 1990)

Powell, W.R.:

—— *John Horace Round: Historian and Gentleman of Essex* (ERO 2001)

—— 1998 'A Revised Bibliography of the Publications of J.H. Round', *Essex Archaeology & History* 29

Renn, D., *Norman Castles in Britain* (John Baker 1968)

Richards, J.D., *Viking Age England* (Tempus new edn. 2000)

Robinson, C.J.:

—— *A History of the Castles of Herefordshire and their Lords* (Longman 1869)

—— *A History of the Mansions and Manors of Herefordshire* (Longman 1972)

Roger of Wendover: *Flowers of History*, trans. Giles, J.A., vol. I, Bohn London 1849 (reprint Llanerch Press 1993)

Round, J.H.:

—— *Feudal England: Historical Studies on the XIth and XIIth Centuries* (Swan Sonnenschein 1909)

—— 'Is Mr. Freeman Accurate?', *The Antiquary* Jun, Oct, Dec 1886

RCHM: Royal Commission on Historical Monuments – Herefordshire 1934

Shoesmith, R., *A Short History of Castle Green and Hereford Castle* (Hereford 1980)

Stafford, P., *Queen Emma & Queen Edith: Queenship and Women's Power in Eleventh-Century England* (Blackwell paperback 2001)

Stenton, F.M., *Anglo-Saxon England*, 3rd edn (OUP 1971)

Stephens, W.R.W., *The Life and Letters of Edward A. Freeman*, vol. I (Macmillan 1895)

Turvey, R., *The Welsh Princes 1063-1283* (Longman 2002)

TWC – Transactions of The Woolhope Club, Herefordshire

VCH: Victoria County History series; letters added denote county. VCHE Essex, VCHH Herefordshire, VCHW Worcestershire

Vita: The Life of King Edward Who Rests at Westminster, (*Vita Eadwardi*) attributed to a monk of Saint-Bertin, ed. & trans. Barlow, F., 2nd edn. (OUP 1992)

Walker, D., 1968 'William fitz Osbern and the Norman Settlement in Herefordshire', *TWC* XXXIX

Walker, I. W., *Harold: The Last Anglo-Saxon King* (Sutton 2004)

Whitelock, D., et. al., *The Norman Conquest: Its setting & Impact* (Eyre & Spottiswoode 1966)

William of Malmesbury:

—— *Gesta Regum Anglorum*, ed. & trans. Mynors, R.A.B., Thomson, R.M. and Winterbottom, M., vol. I (OUP 1998)

—— *The Kings Before the Norman Conquest*, Seeleys London 1853 (reprint Llanerch Press 1989)

—— *The Deeds of the Bishops of England (Gesta Pontificum Anglorum)*, trans Preest D. (Boydell & Brewer 2002)

Williams, A., 1989, 'The king's nephew: the family and career of Ralph, earl of Hereford', *Studies in Medieval History Presented to R. Allen Brown*, eds. C. Harper-Bill, C.J. Holdsworth and J.L. Nelson (Boydell Press 1989)

Index

Other titles published by The History Press

Offa's Dyke
DAVID HILL & MARGARET WORTHINGTON

A mile-by-mile description and new interpretation of the massive linear earthwork along the English-Welsh border, set in the political context of Anglo-Saxon Mercia. Will appeal to academics, amateurs and visitors alike.

ISBN 9780752419589

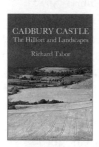

Cadbury Castle: The Hillforts and Landscapes
RICHARD TABOR

Traces the conditions for the development of the Iron Age hillfort at Cadbury Castle, the violent suppression of its population in the first century AD and its major refortification in the post-Roman period. For those interested in Cadbury Castle and hillforts generally.

ISBN 9780752447155

Historic Gardens of Worcestershire
TIMOTHY MOWL

County of a hundred moats, Worcestershire boasts romantic medieval water gardens, stunning landscape parks, enchanted folly towers and many other features reflecting the work of brilliant eccentrics through the years.

ISBN 9780752436546

The Heritage Obsession
BEN COWELL

Our passion for heritage has never been greater. In this book Ben Cowell traces the rise of heritage consciousness in England over the last 300 years, from its origins in the writings of seventeenth-century antiquaries to the present day.

ISBN 9780752440965

Visit our website and discover thousands of other History Press books.

www.thehistorypress.co.uk